# The Narrow Gate
## and
# The Heavenly Footman

# The Narrow Gate

## and

# The Heavenly Footman

John Bunyan

EVANGELICAL PRESS

EVANGELICAL PRESS
Faverdale North Industrial Estate, Darlington, DL3 0PH,
England

Evangelical Press USA
P. O. Box 84, Auburn, MA 01501, USA

e-mail: sales@evangelicalpress.org

web: http://www.evangelicalpress.org

*The Narrow Gate* first published 1676 and *The Heavenly
Footman* first published 1698
This modernized edition first published 2001

**British Library Cataloguing in Publication Data available**

ISBN 0 85234 482 1

Printed and bound in Great Britain by Creative Print &
Design Wales, Ebbw Vale.

# The Narrow Gate

'Strive to enter
through the narrow
gate, for many,
I say to you, will seek
to enter and will not
be able' (Luke 13:24).

# Contents

# The Narrow Gate

## Or the great difficulty of getting to heaven

In this, it is my intention to prove plainly by Scripture, that not only the coarse and profane, but many great who make a profession of faith, will come short of that kingdom.

> Enter by the narrow gate; for wide is the gate and broad is the way that leads to destruction, and there are many who go in by it. Because narrow is the gate and difficult is the way which leads to life, and there are few who find it (Matt. 7:13-14).

### To the reader

Courteous reader,

God, I hope, has put it into my heart to write to you another time, and, at that, about matters of the greatest importance; for now we discourse not about things disputed among the godly, but directly about the saving or damning of the soul. Yes, moreover, this discourse is about the few in number who shall be saved; and it proves that many a person making a great profession of faith will come short of eternal life. For this reason, the matter needs to be sharp and therefore disliked by some; but let it not be rejected by you. The text calls for sharpness; so do the times. Yes, the faithful discharge of my duty towards you has caused me to do it.

I do not now play a tune, but mourn; and it will be well for you if you can graciously lament (Matt. 11:17). Some, they say, make the gate of heaven too wide and some make it too narrow. For my part, I have here presented you with as true a measure of it as I can by the Word of God.

Read me, therefore, yes, read me, and compare me with the Bible. And if you find that my doctrine and that Book of God concur, embrace it, as you will answer for the contrary in the Day of Judgement. This awakening work — if God will make it so — was prepared for you; and if there be the need and it wounds, then get healing by the blood; if it disturbs you, then get peace by the blood; if it takes away all that you have because what you had was naught — for this book is not prepared to take away true grace from anyone — then 'buy from Christ gold refined in the fire, that you may be rich; and white garments that you may be clothed, that the shame of your nakedness may not be revealed; and anoint your eyes with eye salve, that you may see' (Rev. 3:18). Self-flatteries and self-deceptions are easy and pleasant, but damnable. The Lord give you a heart to judge rightly of yourself and of this book, and so to prepare yourself for eternity that you may not only expect to gain entrance, but be received into the kingdom of Christ and of God. Amen.

So prays your friend,

John Bunyan

# I

*Strive to enter through the narrow gate, for many,*
*I say to you, will seek to enter and will not be able*
*(Luke 13:24)*

These are the words of our Lord Jesus Christ, and are there-fore, in a special manner, to be heeded. Besides, the sub-ject matter of the words is the most weighty, that is to say, how we should attain salvation; and therefore should also be heeded. The occasion of the words was a question which one, who at this time was in the company of the disciples, put to Jesus Christ.

The question was this: 'Lord, are there few who are saved?' (Luke 13:23). This was a serious question, but not such as was intended for the destruction of the hearers, as too many nowadays do. Rather this question, as in its own nature, intended the awakening of the company to good, and that called for such an answer as might also profit the people. This question also well pleased Jesus Christ, and he prepared and gave such an answer as was without the least retort or show of distaste. Such an answer, I say, as carried in it the fullest resolve to the question itself, and help to those who were questioning. 'And he said to them, "Strive to enter through the narrow gate, for many, I say to you, will seek to enter and will not be able"' (Luke 13:23-24).

The words are an answer and also an instruction. First, an answer, and that in the affirmative, the gate is *narrow* — many who seek will not be able to enter and therefore only a few shall be saved. Second, the answer is also an instruction: 'Strive to enter, etc.' Good counsel and instruction — may God help me, and my reader, and all who love their salvation to take it. My manner of handling these words will be, first, by way of explanation, and then, second, by way of observation.

## By way of explanation

The words are to be considered, first, with reference to their general meaning and intent, and then, second, with reference to their many and various phrases.

### General meaning

First, the general meaning and intent of the text is to be considered, and that is that great thing — salvation! For these words immediately look at, point to, and give directions about salvation: 'Are there few who are saved?' 'Strive to enter through the narrow gate.' The words, I say, are to direct us not only to talk of, or to wish for, but to understand how we shall, and to seek that we may be effectually saved, and are therefore of the greatest importance. To be saved! What is like being saved? To be saved from sin, from hell, from the wrath of God, from eternal damnation — what is like it? To be made an heir of God, of his grace, of his kingdom and eternal glory — what is like it? And, yet, all this is included in this word *saved*, and in the answer to the question, 'Are there few who are saved?'

Indeed, this word *saved* is but of little use in the world, except to those who are heartily afraid of being damned. This word lies in the Bible, as excellent ointments lie in some men's houses — thrust into a dark place and not thought of for many months because the people of the household have no wounds or sores. In time of sickness, what do we set so much store by as the doctor's vials and containers which are full of his excellent things? But when the person has grown well again, the rest is thrown on the dunghill. Oh, when men are sick of sin and afraid of being damned, what a text is that where the word *saved* is found! Yes, what a word of worth and goodness and blessedness is it to him who lies continually on the wrath of a guilty conscience! 'Those who are well have no need of a physician...' (Matt. 9:12). He therefore, and he only, knows what saved means, who knows what hell and death and damnation mean. 'What must I do to be saved?' (Acts 16:30) is the language of the trembling sinner. 'Lord, save me!' (Matt. 14:30) is the language of the sinking sinner; and none admire the glory that is in the word *saved* but those who see that without being saved all things in heaven and earth are emptiness to them. Those also who believe themselves privileged with all the blessedness that is embodied in that word, bless and admire God who has saved them. Why, since the thing intended, both in the question and in the answer, is no less than the salvation of the soul, I beseech you to 'give the more earnest heed' (Heb. 2:1).

*Particular phrases*

Second, [I] come to the particular phrases in the words and [will] handle them in an orderly way. In the words I find four things:

1. An intimation of the kingdom of heaven;
2. A description of the entrance into it;
3. An exhortation to enter into it;
4. And a motive to enforce that exhortation.

1. *An intimation of the kingdom of heaven*. When he says,
'Strive to enter' — in such phrases there is understood to
be a place, or state, or both to be enjoyed. 'Enter,' enter into
what, or where, but into a state, or place, or both; and therefore when you read this word *enter*, you must say there is
certainly included in the text that good thing that is not
expressed. 'Enter' into heaven where the saved are and shall
be; that is the meaning. Enter into heaven, that place, that
glorious place, where God and Christ and angels are, and
the souls or spirits of 'just men made perfect' (Heb. 12:23).
'Enter' — that thing included, though not expressed in the
words, is called in another text Mount Zion, the heavenly
Jerusalem, the general assembly of the firstborn, who are
written in heaven (Heb. 12:22-23). Therefore, the words
signify to us that there is a state most glorious; and that
will be when this world has ended; and that this place and
state are likewise to be enjoyed and inherited by a generation of men for ever. Besides, this word *enter* signifies that
salvation is to be enjoyed to the full only there, and that
only there is eternal safety to be found. All other places
and conditions are hazardous, dangerous, full of snares,
imperfections, temptations and afflictions. But there, all is
well. There is no devil to tempt, no desperately wicked
heart to deliver us up, no deceitful lust to entangle, nor
any enchanting world to bewitch us. There all shall be well
for all eternity. Furthermore, all the parts of and circum-
stances that accompany salvation are only there to be
enjoyed. There only is immortality and eternal life (2 Cor.
5:1-5); there is the glory and fulness of joy and everlasting

pleasures (Ps. 16:11); there is God and Christ to be seen clearly visible (Heb. 12:22-24); and more, there are the angels and the saints (Luke 20:35-36). Further, there is no death, nor sickness, nor sorrow, nor sighing for ever; there is no pain, nor persecutor, nor darkness to eclipse our glory. Oh, this Mount Zion! Oh, this heavenly Jerusalem!

See therefore what a great thing the Lord Jesus has included by this little word *through*. In this word is embodied a whole heaven and eternal life; even as there is also by other little words in the Holy Scriptures of truth, such as where he says, 'Knock, and it will be opened to you' (Matt. 7:7), and the elect have obtained it. This should teach us not only to read, but to be attentive in reading; not only to read, but to lift up our hearts to God in reading; for if we are not attentive, if he does not give us light and understanding, we may easily pass over, without any great regard for such a word as may have a glorious kingdom and eternal salvation in the essence of it. Yes, sometimes, as in this one, a whole heaven is intimated where it is not at all expressed. The apostles of old were accustomed to drawing out great things from the Scriptures, even out of the very order and timing of the many events and details contained in them. (See Rom. 4:9-11; Gal. 3:16-17; Heb. 8:13.)

2. *A description of the entrance into it.* But, second, as we have here an intimation of the kingdom of heaven, so we have a description of the entrance into it, and by a double illustration at that. (1) It is called a gate. (2) It is called a narrow gate: 'Strive to enter through the narrow gate' (Luke 13:24).

First, it is set forth by the illustration of a gate. A gate, you know, has a double use: it is to open and shut, and so consequently, to let in or to keep out; and to do both of these at the appropriate time. As he said, 'And I said to them, "Do not let the gates of Jerusalem be opened until the sun is hot"' (Neh. 7:3), and again, 'I commanded the gates to be shut, and charged that they must not be opened till after the Sabbath' (Neh. 13:19). And so you find, concerning this gate of heaven, when the five wise virgins came the gate was opened, but afterwards when the other virgins came it was shut (Matt. 25:11-12). So, then, the entrance into heaven is called a gate, to show that there is a time when there may be entrance and that there will come a time when there shall be none. Indeed, this is the principal truth contained in the text: 'Strive to enter through the narrow gate, for many, I say to you, will seek to enter and will not be able' (Luke 13:24). I read in the Scriptures of two gates or doors, through which those who go into heaven must enter.

First, there is the door of faith, the door which the grace of God has opened to the Gentiles (Acts 14:27). This door is Jesus Christ, as also he himself testifies, saying, 'I am the door' (John 10:9). By this door men enter into God's favour and mercy, and find forgiveness through faith in his blood, and live in hope of eternal life; and therefore he himself also has said, 'I am the door. If anyone enters by me, he will be saved' — that is, received into mercy, and given the inheritance of eternal life. But, second, there is another door or gate (for that which is called a gate in the text is twice in the next verse called a door). There is, I say, another gate, and that is the passage into heaven its very self, the entrance into the celestial mansion, and that is the gate mentioned in the text and the door mentioned twice in the verse that follows. And this is what Jacob called it, when he said that Bethel was the house of God and it was the gate of heaven — that is, the entrance — for he saw the entrance into heaven. One end of Jacob's ladder stands in Bethel, God's house, and the other end reaches up to the gate of heaven (Gen. 28:10-18). Jacob's ladder was the figure of Christ. That ladder was not the gate of heaven, but the way from the church to that gate which he saw above at the top of the ladder (Gen. 28:12; John 1:51). But, again, that the gate in the text is the gate or entrance into heaven, consider this: (1) It is that gate that lets men into, or shuts men out of, that place or kingdom where Abraham and Isaac and Jacob are. This place is that paradise where Christ promised the thief that he would be there, the day that he asked to be with him in his kingdom. It is that place into which Paul said he was caught, when he heard words unlawful or impossible for a man to utter (2 Cor. 12:1-6).

*Question*:
But is not Christ the gate or entrance into this heavenly place?
*Answer*:
He is the one without whom no man can get there because by his merits men obtain that world, and also because he (as is the Father) is the donor and dispenser of that kingdom to whom he will. Further, this place is called his house, and he himself the master of it: 'When once the master of the house has risen up and shut the door...' (Luke 13:25). But we are accustomed to saying that the master of the house is not the door. Men enter into heaven by him then, not because he is the gate, or door, or entrance into the celestial mansion, but because he is the giver and dispenser of that kingdom to those whom he shall count worthy of it, because he has obtained it for them.

2. That this gate is the very passage into heaven, consider that the text has special reference to the Day of Judgement when Christ will have laid aside his office as Mediator, which he will have exercised before for the bringing of his

own elect to the faith, and he will then act, not as one who justifies the ungodly, but as one who judges sinners. He will then have risen up from the throne of grace and will shut the door against all the impenitent, and will be seated upon the throne of judgement, from where he will deal with ungodly sinners.

*Objection*:
But Christ bids us to strive: 'Strive [now] to enter through the narrow gate.' But if that gate is, as you say, the gate or entrance into heaven, then it would seem that we should not strive till the Day of Judgement, for we shall not come to that gate until then.

*Answer*:
By this exhortation, 'Strive, etc.', Christ does not at all allow for or countenance delays, or that a man should neglect his own salvation, but instructs weak and feeble men to prepare for the judgement, and counsels them to get those things now that will then give them entrance into glory. This exhortation is much like these: 'Therefore you also be ready, for the Son of Man is coming at an hour you do not expect' (Matt. 24:44) and 'Those who were ready went in with him to the wedding; and the door was shut' (Matt. 25:10). So that when he says, 'Strive to enter,' it is as much as if he should say, 'Blessed are they who shall be admitted another day into the kingdom of heaven; but they who shall be accounted worthy of so unspeakable a favour must be well prepared and fashioned for it beforehand.' Now the time to be fashioned for it is not the Day of Judgement, but the Day of Grace, not then, but now. Therefore, strive now for those things that will then give you entrance into the heavenly kingdom.

But, second, as it is called a gate, so it is called a *narrow* gate: 'Strive to enter through the narrow gate.' The narrowness of this gate is not to be understood in a carnal sense, but in a spiritual sense. You are not to understand it as if the entrance into heaven was some little, pinching wicket gate; no, the narrowness of this gate is quite another thing. This gate is wide enough for all those who are the truly gracious, and sincere lovers of Jesus Christ, but so narrow that not one of the others can by any means enter in: 'Open to me the gates of righteousness; I will go through them, and I will praise the LORD. This is the gate of the LORD, through which the righteous shall enter' (Ps. 118:19-20).

By this word therefore Christ Jesus has shown us that without due qualifications there is no possibility of entering into heaven; the narrow gate will keep all others out. When Christ spoke this parable, he doubtless had in mind some passage or passages from the Old Testament with which the Jews were all acquainted. I will mention two, and so go on.

1. There is the passage in which God turned Adam and his wife out of paradise. Possibly, our Lord might have had his eye upon that; for though that was wide enough for them to go out from, yet it was too narrow for them to go in at. But what should the reason for that be? Why, they had sinned; and therefore 'he placed cherubim at the east of the garden of Eden, and a flaming sword which turned every way, to guard the way to the tree of life' (Gen. 3:24). The cherubim and this flaming sword made the entrance too narrow for them to enter in. Souls, there are cherubim and a flaming sword at the gates of heaven to protect the way to the tree of life; therefore, none but those who are suitably prepared for heaven can enter in at this narrow gate; the

flaming sword will keep all others out: 'Do you not know
that the unrighteous will not inherit the kingdom of God?
Do not be deceived. Neither fornicators, nor idolaters, nor
adulterers, nor homosexuals, nor sodomites, nor thieves,
nor covetous, nor drunkards, nor revilers, nor extortioners
will inherit the kingdom of God' (1 Cor. 6:9-10).

2. Perhaps our Lord might have had in mind the gates of
the temple when he spoke this word to the people; for
though the gates of the temple were six cubits wide, yet
they were so narrow that none who was unclean in any
thing could enter in there (Ezek. 40:48), because placed at
these gates, there were gatekeepers whose office was to see
that none but those who had right to enter could go in there.
And so it is written of Jehoiada that 'he set the gatekeepers
at the gates of the house of the LORD, so that no one who
was in any way unclean should enter' (2 Chron. 23:19).
Souls, God has gatekeepers at the gates of the temple, at the
gate of heaven; gatekeepers, I say, placed there by God to
see that none who is unclean in any thing may come in
there. In at the gate of the church, none may enter now
who is openly profane and scandalous to religion; no,
though they plead that they are beloved of God: 'What has
my beloved to do in my house, having done lewd deeds
with many?' (Jer. 11:15). I say, I am very inclined to believe
that our Lord Jesus Christ had his thoughts upon these two
texts when he said that the gate is narrow; and that which
convinces me all the more is this: a little further on in Luke
chapter 13, he says, 'There will be weeping and gnashing
of teeth, when you see Abraham and Isaac and Jacob and
all the prophets in the kingdom of God, and yourselves
thrust out' (v. 28) — thrust out, which signifies a violent
act, resisting, striving with those who, though they are un-
qualified, would enter. The gatekeepers of the temple were,
for this very thing, to wear arms, if need be, and to be men

of courage and strength, lest the unsanctified or unprepared should by some means enter in. We read in the book of Revelation that the holy city had twelve gates and at the gates [there were] twelve angels. But what did they do there? Why, as well as the rest of their service, this was one of the things: to see that nothing that defiles, or works abomination, and that makes a lie might in any wise enter (Rev. 21:27). But, more particularly, to show [my reader] what it is that makes this gate so narrow, there are three things that make it narrow.

1. There is sin.
2. There is the word of the law.
3. There are the angels of God.

1. There is sin: the sin of the profane, and the sin of the person who professes to be a believer.

First, there is the sin of the profane. But this need not be elaborated upon because it is concluded upon at all hands, that where there is the common belief in the being of God and the judgement to come, 'the wicked shall be turned into hell, and all the nations that forget God' (Ps. 9:17).

Second, but there is the sin of those who make a profession [of faith]; or, consider it rather like this: there is a profession that will stand with an unsanctified heart and life. The sin of such will outweigh the salvation of their souls, the sin-side being the heaviest side of the scale. I say, the heaviest side being the side which has sin in it, they tilt over, and so are, notwithstanding their glorious profession, drowned in ruin and destruction; for none of these has any inheritance in the kingdom of Christ and of God: 'Let no one deceive you with empty words, for because of these things the wrath of God comes upon the sons of disobedience' (Eph. 5:3-6). Neither will a profession of

faith be able to excuse them; the gate will be too narrow for
such as these to enter in there. A man may partake of salvation in part, but not of salvation in full. God saved the
children of Israel out of Egypt, but overthrew them in the
wilderness: 'But I want to remind you, though you once
knew this, that the Lord, having saved the people out of the
land of Egypt, afterwards destroyed those who did not believe' (Jude 5). So we see that, notwithstanding their beginning, 'they could not enter in because of unbelief' (Heb.
3:19).

2. There is the word of the law, and that will make the
gate narrow too. None must go in there but those who can
go in by the permission of the law. For though no man is, or
can be, justified by the works of the law, yet unless the
righteousness and holiness by which he attempts to enter
into this kingdom are justified by the law, it is in vain to
think once of entering in at this narrow gate. Now the law
does not justify; it justifies only on account of the righteousness of Christ. Therefore, if indeed you are not found in
that righteousness, you will find that the law lies just in
the passage into heaven to keep you out. Every man's work
must be tried by fire that it may be made manifest as to
what sort it is. There are two errors in the world about the
law: one is when men think they can enter in at the narrow
gate by the righteousness of the law; the other is when men
think they may enter into heaven without the permission
of the law. Both these, I say, are errors; for as by the works
of the law no flesh shall be justified, so without the consent of the law, no flesh shall be saved: 'For assuredly, I say
to you, till heaven and earth pass away, one jot or one tittle
will by no means pass from the law till all is fulfilled' (Matt.
5:18). He therefore must be damned who cannot be saved
by the consent of the law. And indeed this law is the flaming

sword that turns every way; yes, that lies to this day in the way to heaven, as a bar to all unbelievers and unsanctified professing believers; for it is taken out of the way for only those who have truly found grace. It will be found as a roaring lion to devour all others. Because of the law therefore the gate will be found too narrow for the unsanctified to enter in. When the apostle had told the Corinthians that the unrighteous would not inherit the kingdom of God, and that such were some of them, he adds, 'But you were washed, but you were sanctified, but you were justified in the name of the Lord Jesus and by the Spirit of our God' (1 Cor. 6:11); closely concluding, that had they not been washed, and sanctified, and justified in the name of the Lord Jesus, then, for their transgressions, the law would have kept them out; it would have made the gate too narrow for them to enter in.

3. There are also the angels of God, and by reason of them the gate is narrow. The Lord Jesus calls the end of the world his harvest and says, moreover, that the angels are his reapers. These angels are therefore to gather his wheat into his barn, but to gather the ungodly into bundles to burn them (Matt. 13:39,41,49). Therefore, unless the man who is unsanctified can master the law and conquer angels, unless he can, as I may say, pull them out of the gateway of heaven, he himself will not get there for ever. No man goes to heaven but by the help of the angels — I mean, at the Day of Judgement: 'And he will send his angels with a great sound of a trumpet, and they will gather together his elect from the four winds, from one end of heaven to the other' (Matt. 24:31). If those who shall enter in at the narrow gate shall only be conducted there by the holy angels, when do you think those men will enter in there, concerning whom the angels are commanded to gather, to bind in bundles, to

burn? This therefore is a third difficulty. The angels will make this entrance narrow; yes, too narrow for the unjustified and unsanctified to enter in there.

3. *An exhortation to enter in*. I come now to the exhortation, which is to strive to enter in: 'Strive to enter through the narrow gate.' These words are appropriately added; for as the gate is narrow, it follows then that those who will enter in must strive to do so. 'Strive' — this word *strive* implies:

1. That great idleness is natural to those who profess to be in the faith; they think they can get to heaven by lying, as it were, on their elbows.
2. It also suggests that there will be many difficulties that professing believers will meet with before they get to heaven.
3. It also concludes that only the Christian, man or woman, who labours will get in there. 'Strive, etc.'

I will set forth three questions concerning the word, an answer to which may give us light into the meaning of it:

1. What does the word *strive* imply?
2. How should we strive?
3. Why should we strive?

1. *Question*:
What does this word *strive* imply?
*Answer*:
When he says, 'Strive,' it is as much as to say, incline yourselves towards the work with all your might: 'Whatever your hand finds to do, do it with your might; for there is no work or device or knowledge or wisdom in the grave where you

are going' (Eccles. 9:10). Thus Samson did when he deter-
mined to destroy the Philistines; he bowed himself with all
his might (Judg. 16:30). Thus David did also, when he made
provision for the building and beautifying of the temple of
God (1 Chr. 29:2). And thus must you do, if you are ever to
enter into heaven.

Second, when he says, 'Strive,' he calls for the mind
and will, that they should be on his side and on the side of
the things of his kingdom; for none strive indeed but those
who have given the Son of God their heart, of which the
mind and will are a principal part. For saving conversion
lies more in the turning of the mind and will to Christ, and
to the love of his heavenly things, than in all knowledge
and judgement. And this the apostle confirms when he says,
'Stand fast in one spirit, with one mind, striving...' (Phil. 1:27).

Third, and, more particularly, this word *strive* is expressed by several other terms, such as:

1. It is expressed by these words: 'Run in such a way
that you may obtain it' (1 Cor. 9:24-25).
2. It is expressed by these words: 'Fight the good fight of
faith, lay hold on eternal life' (1 Tim. 6:12).
3. It is expressed by these words: 'Do not labour for the
food which perishes, but for the food which endures to
everlasting life' (John 6:27).
4. It is expressed by these words: 'For we do not wrestle
against flesh and blood, but against principalities, against
powers, against the rulers of the darkness of this age'
(Eph. 6:12).

Therefore, when he says, 'Strive,' it is as much as to say,
'Run for heaven; fight for heaven; labour for heaven; wrestle
for heaven, or you are likely to go without it.'

2. *Question*:

How should we strive?

*Answer*:

The answer in general is: we must strive lawfully: 'And also
if anyone competes in athletics, he is not crowned unless
he competes according to the rules' (2 Tim. 2:5).

*Question:*

But you will say, 'What is it to strive lawfully?'

*Answer*:

(1) To strive against the things which are abhorred by the
Lord Jesus; yes, to resist to the spilling of your blood, striving
against sin (Heb. 12:4). To hold all those things in abomination that are condemned by the Word; yes, though they
are your own right hand, right eye, or right foot; and to
seek by all godly means the utter suppressing of them (Mark
9:43,45,47). (2) To strive lawfully is to strive for those things
that are commanded in the Word: 'But you, O man of God,
flee these things and pursue righteousness, godliness, faith,
love, patience, gentleness. Fight the good fight of faith, lay
hold on eternal life...' (1 Tim. 6:11-12). (3) He who strives
lawfully must therefore be very temperate in all the good
and lawful things of this life: 'And everyone who competes
for the prize is temperate in all things. Now they do it to
obtain a perishable crown, but we for an imperishable
crown' (1 Cor. 9:25). Most of those who make a profession
of faith give permission to the world and the vanity of their
hearts to meet with them and to hang about their necks,
and make their striving to stand rather in an outcry of words
than in a hearty labour against the lusts and love of the
world and their own corruptions; but this kind of striving
is but a beating of the air, and will come to just nothing at
last (1 Cor. 9:26). (4) He who strives lawfully must take God
and Christ along with him as he engages in the work,
otherwise he will certainly be undone: 'To this end I also

labour, striving according to his working which works in me mightily' (Col. 1:29). And for the correct performing of this, he must observe the following particulars: (1) He must take heed that he does not strive about things or words to no profit; for God will not be with him then. 'Remind them of these things,' says the apostle, 'charging them before the Lord not to strive about words to no profit, to the ruin of the hearers' (2 Tim. 2:14). But, alas, how many of those who profess faith in our days are guilty of this transgression, whose religion stands chiefly, if not only, in a few unprofitable questions and vain wranglings about words and things to no profit, but to the destruction of the hearers! (2) He must take heed that whilst he strives against one sin, he does not harbour and shelter another; or, that whilst he cries out against other men's sins, he does not countenance his own. (3) In the striving, strive to believe, strive for the faith of the gospel; for the more we believe the gospel, and the reality of the things of the world to come, with greater strength and courage shall we then labour to possess that blessedness (Phil. 1:27). 'Let us therefore be diligent to enter that rest, lest anyone fall according to the same example of disobedience' (Heb. 4:11). (4) As we should strive for it, and by faith, so should we strive by prayer (Rom. 15:30), by fervent and effectual prayers. Oh, the swarms of our prayerless professing believers! What do they think of themselves? Surely the gate of heaven was previously as wide as it is in our day; but what striving by prayer was there then among Christians for the thing that gives admittance into this kingdom, over and above what there is in these latter days! (5) We should also strive by mortifying our members that are upon the earth: 'Therefore I run thus: not with uncertainty. Thus I fight: not as one who beats the air. But I discipline my body and bring it into subjection, lest, when I have preached to others, I myself should become

disqualified' (1 Cor. 9:26-27). But all this is spoken
principally to those who make a profession of faith; so I
would have it understood.

3. *Question*:
But why should we strive?
*Answer*:
(1) [You should strive] because the thing for which you are
exhorted to strive here is worth the striving for; it is for no
less than a whole heaven and an eternity of happiness there.
How will men strive who have before them a little honour,
a little profit, a little pleasure? I say, again, how will they
strive for this? Now, they do it for a corruptible crown, but
we an incorruptible. I think this word *heaven* and this eternal life truly ought to make us strive; for what is there again
either in heaven or earth like them, to stir a man up to
strive? (2) Strive, because otherwise the devil and hell will
assuredly have you: 'Be sober, be vigilant; because your
adversary the devil walks about like a roaring lion, seeking
whom he may devour' (1 Peter 5:8). These fallen angels are
always watchful, diligent, unwearied; they are also mighty,
subtle, and malicious, seeking nothing more than the damnation of your soul. Oh, strive, you who are like the guile-
less dove! (3) Strive, because every lust strives and wars
against your soul: 'The flesh lusts against the spirit' (Gal.
5:17). 'Beloved, I beg you as sojourners and pilgrims, ab-
stain from fleshly lusts which war against the soul' (1 Peter
2:11). It is a rare thing to see or find a Christian who can
indeed bridle his lusts; but it is no strange thing to see such
professing believers who are not only bridled, but saddled
too, yes, and ridden from lust to sin, from one vanity to
another, by the very devil himself, and the corruptions of
their hearts. (4) Strive, because you have a whole world
against you. The world hates you if you are a Christian; the

men of the world hate you; the things of the world are snares
for you, even your bed and table, your wife and husband;
yes, your most lawful enjoyments have that in them that
will certainly sink your soul to hell, if you do not strive
against the snares that are in them (Rom. 11:9). The world
will seek to keep you out of heaven with its derision, contempt, taunts, threatenings, gaols, gibbets, ropes, burnings,
and a thousand deaths; therefore strive. Again, if it cannot
overcome you with these, it will flatter, promise, allure,
entice, entreat, and use a thousand tricks on this hand to
destroy you; and observe, many who have stood firm against
the threats of the world, have yet been overcome by the
bewitching flatteries of the same. There was ever enmity
between the devil and the church, and between his seed
and her seed too; Michael and his angels, and the dragon
and his angels make war continually (Gen. 3; Rev. 12). There
have been great desires and endeavours among men to
reconcile these two in one, namely, the seed of the serpent
and the seed of the woman; but it has never yet been accom-
plished. The world says, 'They will never come over to us',
and again we say, 'By God's grace, we will never come over
to them.' But the business has not ended in words; both
they and we have also added our endeavours to make each
other submit; but endeavours have proved ineffectual too.
They, for their part, have devised all manner of cruel torments to make us submit, such as slaying with the sword,
stoning, sawing asunder, flames, wild beasts, banishments,
hunger, and a thousand miseries. Again, we, on the other
side, have laboured by prayers and tears, by patience and
long-suffering, by gentleness and love, by sound doctrine
and faithful witness-bearing against their enormities, to
bring them over to us; but yet the enmity remains: so they
must conquer us, or we must conquer them. One side must
be overcome; but the weapons of our warfare are not carnal,

but mighty through God. (5) Strive, because there is nothing
of Christianity gained by idleness: idleness clothes a man
with rags, and the vineyard of the slothful is grown over
with nettles (Prov. 23:21; 24:30-32). A profession of faith
that is not accompanied by spiritual labour cannot bring
the soul to heaven. The fathers before us were not slothful
in business but were 'fervent in spirit, serving the Lord'
(Rom. 12:11). 'That you do not become sluggish, but imi-
tate those who through faith and patience inherit the promises' (Heb. 6:12), strive to enter in. I think that at first reading the words intimate to us that the Christian, in all that
he ever does in this world, should carefully heed and have
regard for his soul; I say, in all that he ever does. Many are
for their souls by fits and starts; but a Christian indeed in
all his doing and designs which he contrives and manages
in this world, should have a special eye to his own future
and everlasting good. In all his labours he should 'strive to
enter': 'Wisdom is the principal thing; therefore get wisdom
[Christ]. And in all your getting, get understanding' (Prov. 4:7).

Get nothing if you cannot get Christ and grace, and
further hopes of heaven in what you are getting. Get nothing with a bad conscience, by hazarding your peace with
God, and that in getting it you weaken your graces which
God has given you; for this is not to 'strive to enter'. Add
grace to grace, both by religious and worldly duties; 'For so
an entrance will be supplied to you abundantly into the
everlasting kingdom of our Lord and Saviour Jesus Christ'
(2 Peter 1:11-12). Religious duties are not the only times for
striving; he who thinks so is out. You may help your faith
and your hope in the godly management of your calling,
and may get further footing in eternal life, by studying the
glory of God in all your worldly activities. I am speaking
now to Christians who are justified freely by grace and am
encouraging, or rather counselling them, to 'strive to enter';

for there is an entering in by faith and good conscience now, as well as our entering in body and soul hereafter; and I must add, that the more your soul is accustomed to enter in by faith now, the more steadfast hope shall you have of entering in hereafter in body and soul: 'Strive to enter.' By these words, also, the Lord Jesus gives sharp rebuke to those professing believers who do not have eternal glory, but other temporal things in their view, by all the noise that they make in the world about religion. There are some, what a stir they make, what a noise and clamour, with their notions and forms! And yet, perhaps, all is for the loaves, because they have eaten of the loaves, and are filled (John 6:26). They strive indeed to enter, but it is not into heaven: they find religion has a good trade at the end of it; or they find that it is the way to credit, repute, advancement, and the like; and therefore they strive to enter into these. But these have not the narrow gate in their view, nor yet have they in themselves love to their poor and perishing souls. For this reason, this exhortation rebukes such, by predicting their damnation: 'Strive to enter.' These words also sharply rebuke those who content themselves, as the angel of the church of Sardis did, namely, 'You have a name that you are alive, but you are dead' (Rev. 3:1), or as those of the church of Laodicea, who took their religion upon trust, and were content with a poor, wretched, lukewarm profession of faith. For such as these do altogether the contrary of the exhortation in the text, which says, 'Strive. Strive to enter'; and they sit and sleep; and they content themselves with a profession that is never likely to bring them there. 'Strive to enter.'

Further, these words make us prove the genuineness of our graces now. For if the narrow gate is the gate of heaven and we are to strive to enter into it now, even while we live and before we get there, then, doubtless, Christ means by this exhortation that we should use all lawful means to prove our graces in this world, whether they will stand in the judgement or not. 'Strive to enter'; get those graces now that will prove to be true graces then; and therefore try those you have; and if, upon trial, they prove not right, cast them away and cry for better, lest they cast you away, when better are not to be had: 'Buy from me gold refined in the fire' (Rev. 3:18). Take note of that. Buy from me faith and grace that will stand in the judgement; strive for that faith; buy from me that grace and also white garments that you may be clothed, that the shame of your wickedness does not appear; and anoint your eyes with eye salve, that you may see. Take to heart this advice; this is the right striving to enter in.

*Question*:
But you will say, 'How should we test our graces? Would you have us run into temptation to test if they are sound or rotten?'
*Answer*:
You need not run into trials. God has ordained that enough of them shall overtake you to prove your graces either rotten or sound before the day of your death. Sufficient for the day is its own evil. If you have but a sufficiency of grace to withstand, I say, you shall have enough trials overtaking you, to prove your graces sound or rotten. If God shall help you, you may therefore see how it is likely to be with you before you go out of this world, namely, whether your graces are such as will carry you in at the gates of heaven or not.

*Question*:
But how should we try our graces now?
*Answer*:
How do you find them in outward trials? (See Heb. 11:15-16). How do you find yourself in the inward workings of sin?

(Rom. 7:24). How do you find yourself under the highest enjoyment of grace in this world? (Phil. 3:14).

*Question*:
But what do you mean by these three questions?
*Answer*:
I mean graces show themselves at these times and seasons, whether they are rotten or sound.

*Question*:
How do they show themselves to be true under the first of these?
*Answer*:
They do this by mistrusting their own sufficiency; by crying to God for help (2 Chr. 14:11; 20:12); by desiring rather to die than to bring any dishonour to the name of God (Acts 4; 20:22); and by considering that, if God is honoured in the trial, they have gained more than all the world could give them (2 Cor. 4:17-18; Heb. 11:24-25).

*Question*:
How do they show themselves to be true under the second?
*Answer*:
They do this by mourning, and confessing (Zech. 12:10), and striving, and praying against them (Heb. 12:4); by not being content, should they have heaven, if they live and defile them (Ps. 19:12); and by esteeming holiness to be the greatest beauty in the world; and by flying to Jesus Christ for life (John 19).

*Question*:
How do they show themselves to be true under the third?
*Answer*:
They do this by prizing the true graces above all the world; by praying heartily that God will give them more; by not

being content with all the grace they can be capable of enjoying on this side of heaven and glory (Ps. 84:10; Luke 17:5; Phil. 3).

'Strive to enter.' The reason why Christ adds these words *to enter* is obvious, namely, because there is no true and lasting happiness on this side of heaven. I say, none that is both true and lasting (I mean as to our senses and feeling, as there shall be) for here we have no continuing city, but we seek one to come (Heb. 13:14). Heaven is within; strive therefore to enter in: the glory is within; strive therefore to enter in: Mount Zion is within; strive therefore to enter in: the heavenly Jerusalem is within; strive therefore to enter in: angels and saints are within; strive therefore to enter in: and to make up all, the God and Father of our Lord Jesus Christ, and that glorious Redeemer are within; strive therefore to enter in.

'Strive to enter.' For without are dogs, sorcerers, and the sexually immoral, and murderers, and idolaters, and whoever loves and practises a lie (Rev. 22:15). Without are also demons, and hell, and death, and all damned souls (Matt. 25:41; Rev. 12:9). Without is howling, weeping, wailing, and gnashing of teeth (Isa. 65:13-14; Matt. 22:13). Yes, without are all the miseries, sorrows, and plagues that an infinite God can in justice and power inflict upon an evil and wicked generation (Deut. 29:18-20): 'Strive to enter through the narrow gate.' 'Strive to enter through the narrow gate, for many, I say to you, will seek to enter and will not be able' (Luke 13:24).

*4. A motive to enforce that exhortation.* We have now come to the motivation which our Lord urges to enforce his exhortation. He told us before that the gate is narrow; he also exhorted us to strive to enter in there, or to get those things now that will further our entrance then, and to set ourselves against those things that will hinder our entering in. In this motivation there are five things to be kept in mind. (1) There will be disappointment for some on the Day of Judgement; for many will seek to enter in, and shall not be able. (2) Not a few, but many, will meet with this disappointment; for many will seek to enter in, and shall not be able. (3) This doctrine of the falling short of many then stands upon the validity of the word of Christ: 'For many, I say to you, will seek to enter and will not be able.' (4) Those who have made a profession of faith shall form a great crowd among the many who shall fall short of heaven: 'For many, I say to you, will seek to enter and will not be able.' (5) Where grace and striving are lacking now, seeking and contending to enter in will be unprofitable then: 'For many, I say to you, will seek to enter and will not be able.'

But I will proceed in my former method, namely, to explain the words to you. 'For many, etc.' If he had said, 'For some will fall short,' it would have been a sentence to be remembered. If he had said, 'For some who seek will fall short,' it would have been very awakening. But when he says, 'Many, many will fall short, yes, many among professing believers will fall short,' this is not only awakening, but dreadful. 'For many, etc.'; I find this word applied in various ways in Scripture.

1. Sometimes it means the openly profane, the wicked and ungodly world, such as where Christ says, 'Wide is the gate and broad is the way that leads to destruction, and there are many who go in by it' (Matt. 7:13). I say, by the many here, he means chiefly those who go on in the broad way of sin and profaneness, bearing the tokens of their damnation on their foreheads (Isa. 3:9); those whose daily practice proclaims that their feet go down to death, and their steps take hold of hell (Job 21:29-30; Prov. 4).

2. Sometimes this word *many* means those who cleave to the people of God deceitfully and in hypocrisy, or, as Daniel has it, 'Many shall join with them by intrigue' (Dan. 11:34). The word *many* in this text includes all those who make pretence of being better than they are in religion. It includes, I say, those who have religion only for a holy-day suit to give them prominence at certain times, and when they come among suitable company.

3. Sometimes this word *many* means those who apostatize from Christ, such as those who for a while believe and then in time of temptation fall away, as John says of some of Christ's disciples, 'From that time many of his disciples went back and walked with him no more' (John 6:66).

4. Sometimes this word *many* means those who make a great noise and do many great things in the church, and yet lack saving grace: 'Many,' says Christ, 'will say to me in that day, "Lord, Lord, have we not prophesied in your name, cast out demons in your name, and done many wonders in your name?"' (Matt. 7:22). Take note, there will be many of these.

5. Sometimes this word *many* means those poor, ignorant, deluded souls who are led away with every wind of doctrine; those who are caught by the cunning and crafty deceiver, who lies in wait to beguile the unstable: 'And many will follow their destructive ways, because of whom the way of truth will be blasphemed' (2 Peter 2:2).

6. Sometimes this word *many* includes all the world, good and bad: 'And many of those who sleep in the dust of the earth shall awake, some to everlasting life, some to shame and everlasting contempt' (Dan. 12:2; compare this with John 5:28-29).

7. Lastly, sometimes this word *many* refers to the good only: those who shall be saved (Luke 1:16; 2:34).

Then, since the word is applied so variously, let us inquire as to how it must be taken in the text. (1) It must not
be applied to the sincerely godly, for they shall never perish
(John 10:27-28). (2) It cannot be applied to all the world,
for then no flesh should be saved. (3) Neither is it to be
applied to the openly profane only, for then the hypocrite
is by it excluded. (4) But by the *many* in the text our Lord
refers, in particular, to the one who claims to be a believer,
the one who makes a profession of faith. I say, however
high he may seem now, he shall be found without saving
grace in the Day of Judgement. Now that the one who claims
to be a believer, in particular, is intended in this text, consider this: as soon as the Lord had said, 'Many ... will seek
to enter and will not be able,' he pointed, as with his finger,
at the many who he, then, in particular intended, namely,
those among whom he had taught; those who had eaten
and drunk in his presence (Luke 13:26); those who had
prophesied and cast out demons in his name, and in his
name had done many wonderful works (Matt. 7:27). These
are the *many* intended by the Lord in this text, though others
are also included under the sentence of damnation by his
word in other passages: 'For many...' Concerning this
narrow gate, Matthew says that there are but few who find
it. But it seems the castaways in my text found it; for you
read that they knocked at it and cried, 'Lord, Lord open for
us.' So then, the meaning may seem to be this: many of the
few who find it will seek to enter in, and shall not be able.

I find at the Day of Judgement that some will be crying
to the rocks to cover them, and some will be crying at the
gates of heaven for entrance. Suppose that those who cry
to the rocks to cover them are those whose consciences
will not allow them once to look God in the face, because
they have fallen under present guilt and the dreadful fears
of the wrath of the Lamb (Rev. 6:16); and that those who

stand crying at the gate of heaven are those whose confidence holds out to the last — even those whose boldness
will enable them to contend even with Jesus Christ for
entrance; those, I say, who will have a profession of faith,
the casting out of demons, and the performing of many
wonderful works to plead. Of this sort are the *many* in my
text: 'For many, I say to you, will seek to enter and will not
be able.' 'For many, etc.' Could we compare the professing
believers of these times with the everlasting Word of God,
this doctrine would more easily appear to the children of
men. How few among the many, yes, among the swarms of
those who profess faith, have the heart to make it a matter
of conscience to walk before God in this world, and to study
his glory among the children of men! How few, I say, have
his name lie nearer their hearts than their own carnal concerns! No, how few do not make his Word, his name, and
his ways a guise for their own worldly advantages! God
calls for faith (Mark 11:22); good conscience (1 Peter 3:16);
moderation (Heb. 13:5); self-denial (Matt. 10:37-39); humility (Phil. 4:5); heavenly-mindedness (Col. 3:1-4); love to
the saints (John 15:17; 1 John 4:21), to enemies (Matt. 5:44);
and for conformity in heart (Prov. 23:26), in word (Col. 4:6),
and life (Rev. 2:10) to his will (Micah 6:8). But where is it?

'For many, I say to you.' These latter words carry in them
a double argument to prove the truth asserted before. First,
in that he directly pointed at his followers: 'I say to you.'
'Many, I say to you, even to you who are my disciples, to
you who have eaten and drunk in my presence.' I know
that sometimes Christ has directed his speech to his
disciples, not so much upon their account, as upon account
of others. But here it is not so; the 'I say to you' in this text
immediately concerned some of them: 'I say to you...You
shall begin to stand outside and to knock at the door, saying,
"Lord, Lord, open for us," and he will answer and say to

you, "I do not know you, where you are from." Then you will begin to say, "We ate and drank in your presence, and you taught in our streets." But he will say, "I tell you, I do not know you, where you are from. Depart from me, all you workers of iniquity. It is *you*, *you*, *you* that I mean. 'I say to you.'"' It is common with a professing people, when they hear a sharp and thundering sermon, to say, 'Now has the preacher not paid off the drunkard, the swearer, the liar, the covetous, the adulterer,' forgetting that these sins may be committed in a spiritual and mystical way. There is spiritual drunkenness, spiritual adultery; and a man may be a liar who calls God his Father when he is not, or who calls himself a Christian, when he is not.

Why, perhaps all these thunders and lightnings in this terrible sermon may concern you more than you are aware of it: 'I say to you, to you who profess to be believers. May the application of all this thunder be to you?' (Rev. 2:9; 3:9). Had the Lord Jesus not intended by these words to show what an overthrow will one day be made among those who profess to be believers, he need not have included the *you* in it at this rate — as in the text, and afterwards he has done so. The sentence would make sense enough without it, I say, without his saying, 'I say to you'. But the truth is, the professing believer is in danger; the preacher and the hearer, the workers of miracles, and workers of wonders may all be in danger of damning, notwithstanding all their achievements. And to awaken us all to this truth therefore the text must run like this: 'For many, I say to you, will seek to enter and will not be able.' Do you not yet see that the person who makes a profession of faith is in danger, and that these words, 'I say to you,' are a prophecy of the everlasting ruin of some who are famous in the congregation of saints? I say, if you do not see it, may it please God to open your eyes. Take heed that your portion is not the portion of one of those who are described in verse 28 of Luke chapter 13: 'There will be weeping and gnashing of teeth, when you see Abraham and Isaac and Jacob and all the prophets in the kingdom of God, and yourselves thrust out.' 'For many, I say to you.' I told you, these words carry in them a double argument for confirmation of the truth asserted before.

First, those who profess faith are particularly pointed at here; and, second, it is the saying of the one who is truth himself. For these words, 'I say,' are words full of authority; 'I say it; I say to you,' says Christ, as he says in another text: 'It is I who speak; behold, it is I.' The person whose words we now have under consideration was no blundering raw-headed preacher, he was the very wisdom of God, his Son, and he who has lain in his bosom from everlasting, and consequently, had the most perfect knowledge of his Father's will, and how it would fare with those who professed faith at the end of this world. And, now, hear what he says of the words which he has spoken, 'Heaven and earth will pass away, but my words will by no means pass away' (Matt. 24:35). 'I say to you.'

The prophets used not to speak in this manner, nor even the holy apostles; for to speak in this way is to indicate that things should be received upon their own authority. They were accustomed to saying, 'Thus says the Lord, or Paul, or Peter, an apostle, or a servant of God.' But now we are dealing with the words of the Son of God; it is he who has said it. Thus we find the truth of the perishing of many who make a profession of faith asserted and confirmed by Christ's own mouth. This consideration carries great awakening power in it; but many have fallen into such a fast sleep nowadays that nothing will awaken them except that shrill and terrible cry, 'Behold, the bridegroom is coming; go out to meet him!' (Matt. 25:6).

'I say to you.' There are two things upon which this assertion may be grounded. (1) There is a thing in the world like grace, that is not grace. (2) There is a sin called the sin against the Holy Spirit, from which there is no redemption. And both these things come upon those who profess to be believers.

First, there is a thing in the world like grace, that is not grace. That is evident because we read that there are some who not only make a fair show in the flesh (Gal. 6:12), who glory in appearance (2 Cor. 5:12), who appear beautiful outwardly (Matt. 23:27), who do as God's people do, but have not the grace of God's people (Isa. 57:3-4). It is evident also from those frequent cautions about this thing which are given to us everywhere in the Scriptures: 'Do not be deceived' (Gal. 6:7); 'Let a man examine himself' (1 Cor. 11:28); 'Examine yourselves as to whether you are in the faith' (2 Cor. 13:5). All these expressions intimate to us that there may be a show of, or a thing like grace, where there is no grace indeed.

Second, this is evident from the conclusion made by the Holy Spirit about this very thing: 'For if anyone thinks himself to be something, when he is nothing, he deceives himself' (Gal. 6:3). The Holy Spirit here concludes that a man may think himself to be something; may think he has grace, when he has none, may think himself something for heaven and another world, when indeed he is just nothing at all with reference to it. Upon this point, the Holy Spirit also determines, namely, that those who do so deceive themselves, 'For if anyone thinks himself to be something, when he is nothing, he deceives himself' (Gal. 6:3), they deceive their own souls; they deceive themselves of salvation: 'Let no one cheat you of your reward' (Col. 2:18).

Third, it is clear from the text: 'For many, I say to you, will seek to enter and will not be able' (Luke 13:24). Alas, great light, great ability, great works, and great confidence of heaven may be where there is not the faith of God's elect, no love of the Spirit, no repentance leading to salvation, no sanctification of the Spirit, and so consequently, no saving grace!

2. But, as there is a thing like grace which is not grace, so is there a sin, called the sin against the Holy Spirit, from which there is no redemption; and this sin does more than ordinarily overcome those who claim to have faith.

There is a sin called the sin against the Holy Spirit, from which there is no redemption. This is evident both from Matthew and Mark: 'Anyone who speaks a word against the Son of Man, it will be forgiven him; but whoever speaks against the Holy Spirit, it will not be forgiven him, either in this age or in the age to come' (Matt. 12:32; Mark 3:29). For this reason, when we know that a man has sinned this sin, we are not to pray for him, or to have compassion on him (1 John 5:16; Jude 22). This sin usually befalls those who profess to be believers; for there are few, if any, who make no profession of faith, who are at present capable of sinning this sin. 'Those who were once enlightened, and have tasted the heavenly gift, and have become partakers of the Holy Spirit, and have tasted the good word of God and the powers of the age to come' (Heb. 6:4-5); this is the sort who commit this sin. Peter also describes them as being those who sin the unpardonable sin: 'For if, after they have escaped the pollutions of the world through the knowledge of the Lord and Saviour Jesus Christ, they are again entangled in them and overcome, the latter end is worse for them than the beginning' (2 Peter 2:20). The other passage in chapter 10 of Hebrews holds forth the same thing: 'For if we sin willfully after we have received the knowledge of the truth, there no longer remains a sacrifice for sins, but a certain fearful expectation of judgement, and fiery indignation which will devour the adversaries' (vv. 26-27). These therefore are the persons who are the prey for this sin: this sin feeds upon those who profess faith, and they who are such, do very often fall into the mouth of this eater. Some fall into the mouth of this sin by delusions and doctrines of demons; and some fall into the mouth of it by returning with the dog to his own vomit, and with the sow that was washed to her wallowing in the mire (2 Peter 2:22). I shall not give you a particular description of this sin here — that I have done elsewhere — but such a sin there is, and those who commit it shall never have forgiveness. And, I say, again, there are those who profess faith who commit this unpardonable sin; yes, more than most are aware of. Let all therefore look to themselves. May the Lord awaken them to do so; for what with a profession without grace and by the venom of the sin against the Holy Spirit, many will seek to enter in, and shall not be able. 'Will seek to enter' — this kingdom, at the gate of which the reprobate will be stopped — this kingdom which will be the desire of all the world at the last judgement; and they, especially those in my text, will seek to enter in; for then they will see that the blessedness is for those who get into this kingdom, according to that which is written: 'Blessed are those who do his commandments, that they may have the right to the tree of life, and may enter through the gates into the city' (Rev. 22:14). To prove to you that they will seek, although I have done it already, read these texts at your leisure: Matthew 25:11; Matthew 7:22; Luke 13:28. And, in a word, to give you the reason why they will seek to enter in.

First, then they will see what a kingdom it is, what glory there is in it; and then they shall also see the blessedness which they who shall then be counted worthy to enter in shall have. The reason why this kingdom is so little regarded is because it is not seen; the glory of it is hid from the eyes of the world: '[Their] eye has not seen, nor [their] ear heard, etc.' Yes, but then they shall hear and see too; and when this comes to pass, then, even then, he who now most seldom thinks of it will seek to enter in.

Second, they will then see what hell is and what damnation there is in hell more clearly than ever. They will also see how the breath of the Lord, like a stream of brimstone, kindles it. Oh, the sight of the burning fiery furnace, which is prepared for the devil and his angels! This, this will incite work in the souls of castaways at that day of God Almighty, and then they will seek to enter in.

Third, then they will see what the meanings of words, such as these are: hell-fire, everlasting fire, devouring fire, fire that never shall be quenched. Then they will see what *for ever* means, what *eternity* means; then they will see what this word *the bottomless pit* means; then they will hear roaring of sinners in this place, howling in that, some crying to the mountains to fall upon them, and others to the rocks to cover them; then they will see blessedness is nowhere but within heaven.

Fourth, then they will see what glory the godly are possessed with: how they rest in Abraham's bosom; how they enjoy eternal glory; how they walk in their white robes; and are equal to the angels. Oh, the favour and blessedness and unspeakable happiness that God's people shall then have; and this shall be seen by those who are shut out, by those whom God has rejected for ever; and this will make them seek to enter in (Luke 16:22-23). 'Will seek to enter' (Luke 13:24).

*Question*:
But some may say, 'How will they seek to enter in?'

*Answer:*

(1) They will put on all the confidence they can; they will trick and trim up their profession, and adorn it with what bravery they can. In this way, the foolish virgins sought to enter in. They did trim their lamps, make themselves as fine as they could. They sought a ruse to make their lamps shine awhile; but the Son of God revealing himself, their confidence failed, their lamps went out, the door was shut upon them, and they were kept out. (2) They will seek to enter in by crowding themselves in among the godly. In this manner, the man without the wedding garment sought to enter in: he goes to the wedding, gets into the wedding-chamber, sits close among the guests, and then, without doubt, concluded he would escape damnation. But, you know, one black sheep is soon seen, though it is among a hundred white ones. Why, it fared even thus with this poor man: and when the king came in to see the guests, he saw a man there who did not have on a wedding garment. He spied him presently, and before one word was spoken to any of the others, he had this dreadful greeting, 'Friend, how did you come in here without having a wedding garment on?' And he was speechless; though he could wax eloquent among the guests, yet the master of the feast, at first coming in, strikes him dumb; and having nothing to say for himself, the king had something to say against him: 'Then the king said to the servants [the angels], "Bind him hand and foot, take him away, and cast him into outer darkness; there will be weeping and gnashing of teeth"' (Matt. 22:13). (3) They will seek to enter in by pleading their profession [of faith] and admittance to the Lord's ordinances when they were in the world: 'Then you will begin to say, "We ate and drank in your presence, and you taught in our streets"' (Luke 13:26). 'We sat at your table, and used to frequent sermons and Christian assemblies; we were well

thought of by your saints, and were admitted into your
churches; we professed the same faith as they did; "Lord,
Lord, open to us."' (4) They will seek to enter in by pleading
their virtues: how they were subject to his ministry; how
they were sanctified for him; what good they did in the
world, and the like (Matt. 7:22). But neither will this help
them; the same answer that the two former had, the same
have these: 'Depart from me, all you workers of iniquity'
(Luke 13:27). (5) They will seek to enter in by pleading
excuses, when they cannot evade conviction. The slothful
servant did exactly this when he was called to account for
not improving his Lord's money: 'Lord,' says he, 'I knew
you to be a hard man, reaping where you have not sown,
and gathering where you have not scattered seed. And I
was afraid, etc. [either that I should not please in laying
out your money, or that I should put it into hands out of
which I should not get it again when you required it] and
went and hid your talent in the ground. Look, there you
have what is yours' (Matt. 25:24-25). As if he had said, 'True,
Lord, I have not improved; I have not got. But consider
also, I have not embezzled; I have not spent nor lost your
money. Lo, there you have what is yours' (Matt. 25:24-28).
There are but few who will be able to say these last words
at the Day of Judgement. Most of those who profess faith
are for embezzling, misspending, and wasting away their
time, their talents, their opportunities for doing good. But,
I say, if he who can make so good an excuse as to say, 'Look,
there you have what is yours', I say, if such a one shall be
called a wicked and slothful servant; if such a one shall be
put to shame at the Day of Judgement; yes, if such a one
shall, notwithstanding this care to save his Lord's money,
be cast as unprofitable into utter darkness, where there shall
be weeping and gnashing of teeth, what will those do who

have neither taken care to make use of, nor care to keep what was committed to their trust? (6) They will seek to enter in by pleading that ignorance was the ground of their falling short in the things where they offended. It is for this reason, when Christ charges them with lack of love for him and with an absence of those fruits that should prove their love to be true, such as that they did not feed him, did not give him drink, did not take him in, did not clothe him, visit him, come to him, and the like, they readily reply, 'Lord, when did we see you hungry or thirsty or a stranger or naked or sick or in prison, and did not minister to you?' (Matt. 25:44). As if to say, 'Lord, we are not conscious in ourselves that this charge is worthily laid at our door. God forbid that we should have been such sinners. But, Lord, give an instance, when did it occur, or where? True, there was a company of poor, sorry people in the world, very inconsiderable, esteemed by nobody; but as for you, we professed you, we loved you; and had you been with us in the world, you would have worn gold, you would have eaten the sweetest of the world, we would have provided it for you; and therefore "Lord, Lord, open to us."' But will this plea do? No, then shall he answer them, 'Inasmuch as you did not do it to one of the least of these, you did not do it to me' (Matt. 25:45). This plea, then, though grounded upon ignorance, which is one of the strangest pleas for neglect of duty, would not give them admittance into the kingdom: 'These will go away into everlasting punishment, but the righteous into eternal life' (v. 46).

I might add other things which will indicate how they will seek to enter in. As, (1) they will stop at this gate, this beautiful gate of heaven; they will begin to stand outside the gate, as being loath to go any further. Never did a malefactor so unwillingly turn off the ladder when the rope

was about his neck, as these will turn away in that Day
from the gates of heaven to hell. (2) They will not only stop
at the gate, but there they will knock and call. This also
shows them willing to enter. They will begin to stand outside and to knock at the gate, saying, 'Lord, Lord, open to
us.' This word *Lord* being repeated shows the vehemency
of their desires: 'Lord, Lord, open to us; the demons are
coming; Lord, Lord, the pit opens her mouth upon us; Lord,
Lord, there is nothing but hell and damnation left to us, if,
Lord, Lord, you have not mercy upon us; Lord, Lord, open
to us.'

Third, their last argument for entrance is their tears.
When groundless confidence, pleading of virtues, excuses,
and ignorance will not do; when standing at the gate,
knocking and calling, 'Lord, Lord, open to us,' will not do;
then they give themselves to their tears. Tears are sometimes the most powerful arguments, but they are worth
nothing here. Esau also sought it carefully with tears, but it
helped him nothing at all (Heb. 12:15-17). There shall be
weeping and gnashing of teeth; for the gate is shut for ever;
mercy is gone for ever; Christ has rejected them for ever.
All their pleas, excuses, and tears will not make them able
to enter into this kingdom. 'For many, I say to you, will
seek to enter and will not be able.'

I come now to the latter part of the words which closely
show us the reason of the rejection of these many who must
be damned — they 'will seek to enter, and will not be able'.

Hypocrites, false believers, may go a great way; they may
pass through the first and second watch — that is, may be
approved by Christians and churches; but what will they
do when they come to this iron gate that leads into the
city? There the workers of iniquity will fall, be cast down,
and shall not be able to rise.

'And will not be able.' The time, as I have already hinted, which my text concerns is the Day of Judgement, a day when all masks and disguises shall be taken off from all faces. It is a day when God 'will both bring to light the hidden things of darkness and reveal the counsels of the hearts' (1 Cor. 4:5). It is also the day of his wrath, the day in which he will pay vengeance, even a recompense to his adversaries. At this day, those things that now these 'many' may count sound and good will then shake like a quagmire, even all their naked knowledge, their feigned faith, pretended love, glorious shows of gravity in the face, their holy-day words, and pleasing deportment will stand them in little stead. I call them holy-day ones, for I perceive that some professing believers do with religion just as people do with their best clothing: hang it against the wall all the week and put it on on Sundays. For as some hardly ever put on a suit except when they go to a fair or a market, so little house religion will be acceptable to some; they save religion till they go to a meeting, or till they meet with a godly pedlar. O poor religion! O poor professing believer! What will you do on this day, and the day of your trial and judgement? Cover yourself you cannot; pass for a Christian you cannot; stand against the Judge you cannot. What will you do? 'The ungodly shall not stand in the judgement, nor sinners in the congregation of the righteous' (Ps. 1:5). 'And will not be able' — the ability referred to here is not that which stands in carnal power of fleshly subtlety, but in the truth and simplicity of those things for the sake of which God gives the kingdom of heaven to his people.

There are five things for the lack of which these people will not be able to enter.

1. This kingdom belongs to the elect, to those for whom it was prepared from the foundation of the world

(Matt. 25:34). Hence, Christ says that when he comes, he will send forth his angels with a great sound of a trumpet and they shall gather together his elect from the four winds, from one end of heaven to another (Matt. 24:31). And hence, he says again, 'I will bring forth descendants from Jacob, and from Judah an heir of my mountains; my elect shall inherit it, and my servants shall dwell there' (Isa. 65:9). 'If it were possible, they shall deceive the very elect' (Matt. 24:24, AV). 'But the elect have obtained it, and the rest were blinded' (Rom. 11:7).

2. They will not be able to enter because they will lack the birthright. The kingdom of heaven is for the heirs, and if children, then heirs; if born again, then heirs. For this reason, it is said expressly, 'Except a man be born again, he cannot see the kingdom of God' (John 3:3, AV). By this one word, down goes all carnal privilege of being born of flesh and blood, and of the will of man. Can you produce the birthright? But are you sure you can? For it will be of little profit to you to think of the blessed kingdom of heaven, if you lack a birthright to give you an inheritance there. Esau despised his birthright, saying, 'What good will this birthright do me?' And there are many of his mind in the world to this day. 'Tush,' they say, 'they talk of being born again; what good shall a man get by that?' They say, 'No going to heaven without being born again. But God is merciful; Christ died for sinners; and we will turn when we can attend to it, and doubt not but all will be well at last.' But I will answer you, child of Esau, the birthright and blessing go together; miss of one, and you shall never have the other. Esau found this to be true; for having first despised the birthright, when he would afterwards have inherited the blessing, he was rejected; for he found no place for repentance, though he sought it carefully with tears (Gen. 25:29-34; Heb. 12:16-17).

3. They shall not be able to enter in who have not believed with the faith wrought upon them by God; the faith that is most holy, even the faith of God's elect: 'He who believes in the Son has everlasting life; and he who does not believe the Son shall not see life, but the wrath of God abides on him' (John 3:36). But now, this faith is the effect of electing love and of a new birth (John 1:11-13). Therefore, all those who make a profession of faith but who have not that faith which flows from being born of God, will seek to enter in, and shall not be able.

4. They shall not be able to enter in who have not gospel holiness. Holiness which is the effect of faith is that which admits into the presence of God and into his kingdom too: 'Blessed and holy is he who has part in the first resurrection. Over such, the second death [which is hell and eternal damnation] has no power' (Rev. 20:6,14) — blessed and holy, with the holiness that flows from faith which is in Christ; for to these the inheritance belongs: 'That they may receive forgiveness of sins and an inheritance among those who are sanctified by faith in me,' says Christ (Acts 26:18). This holiness which is the natural effect of faith in the Son of God, Christ Jesus the Lord will, at this Day of Judgement, distinguish from all other shows of holiness and sanctity, be they what they will, and will admit the soul that has this holiness into his kingdom, when the rest will seek to enter in, and shall not be able.

5. They shall not be able to enter in who do not persevere in this blessed faith and holiness. Not that they who have them indeed can finally fall away and everlastingly perish; but it has pleased Jesus Christ to bid those who have the right to hold fast that they have, to endure to the end; and then tells them they shall be saved — though it is as true that none has the power to keep himself; but God works together with his children; and they are kept by the

power of God, through faith for salvation, which is also laid up in heaven for them (1 Peter 1:3-5). 'The boastful shall not stand in your sight; you hate all workers of iniquity' (Ps. 5:5). The boastful are the ungodly ones, who have neither faith, nor holiness, nor perseverance in godliness, and yet lay claim to the kingdom of heaven; but, 'better is a little with righteousness, than vast revenues without justice' (Prov. 16:8). What is it for me to claim a house, or a farm, without right? Or to say, 'All this is mine, but have nothing to show for it?' This is just like the revenues of the foolish: his estate lies in his conceit; he has nothing by birthright and law, and therefore shall not be able to inherit the possession: 'For many, I say to you, will seek to enter and will not be able.' Thus you can see that the nonelect shall not be able to enter; that he who is not born again shall not be able to enter; that he who has not saving faith, with holiness and perseverance flowing out from it, shall not be able to enter. For this reason, consider what I have said.

# II

I come now to give you some observations from the words, and they may be three

> 1. When men have put in all the claim they can for heaven, but few will have it for their inheritance: 'For many, I say to you, will seek to enter and will not be able.'
> 2. Great therefore will be the disappointment that many will meet with at the Day of Judgement: 'For many, I say to you, will seek to enter, and will not be able.'
> 3. Going to heaven therefore will be no trivial business; salvation is not obtained by a dream; those who would then have that kingdom, must now strive lawfully to enter: 'For many, I say to you, will seek to enter and will not be able.'

I shall speak chiefly, and yet briefly, to the first of these observations, namely, that when men have put in all the claim they can to the kingdom of heaven, but few will have it for their inheritance. The observation stands in two parts. (1) The time is coming, when every man will put in whatever claim he can to the kingdom of heaven. (2) There will be but few of those who put in a claim for it who shall enjoy it for their inheritance.

First, I shall speak but a word or two to the first part of
the observation because I have previously presented my
treatment of it by my exposition of the words. But you find
in chapter 25 of Matthew that all those who are on the left
hand of the Judge put in all the claim they could for this
blessed kingdom of heaven. If you should consider those
on the left hand, as most do, to be all the sinners that shall
be damned, then that completely proves the first part of
the observation; for it is expressly said, 'Then they also [all
of them jointly, and every one individually] will answer
him, saying, "Lord, when did we see you hungry or thirsty
or a stranger or naked or sick or in prison, and did not
minister to you?"' (Matt. 25:44). Here I could bring in the
plea of the slothful servant, the cry of the foolish virgins; I
could also give some exposition on that passage here: 'We
ate and drank in your presence, and you taught in our
streets' (Luke 13:26). But these things I have handled
already, in the handling of which the first part of the observation has been proved; for this reason, without more words,
I will, God assisting by his grace, move on to the second
part of it, namely, there will be but few of those who put in
a claim for it who will enjoy it for their inheritance. I shall
speak distinctly to this part of the observation and shall
first confirm it by a scripture or two.

'Narrow is the gate and difficult is the way which
leads to life, and there are few who find it' (Matt. 7:14).

'Do not fear, little flock, for it is your Father's good
pleasure to give you the kingdom' (Luke 12:32).

By these two texts, and by many more that will be quoted
anon, you may see the truth of what I have said.

[I shall] enlarge therefore upon the truth; and, in the first instance, more generally; and, in the second, more particularly.

(1) More generally, I shall prove that in all ages only a few have been saved. (2) More particularly, I shall prove that only a few of them who profess faith have been saved.

First, in the old world, when it was most populous, even in the days of Noah, we read of only eight persons who were saved out of it. Therefore, Peter might well call them but few. But how few? Why, only eight souls: 'In which a few, that is, eight souls, were saved through water' (1 Peter 3:20). He touches a second time upon this truth, saying, 'And did not spare the ancient world, but saved Noah, one of eight people, a preacher of righteousness, bringing in the flood on the world of the ungodly' (2 Peter 2:5). Take note, all the rest are called the ungodly, and there was also a world of them. These are also taken notice of in Job, and are referred to there also by the name of wicked men: 'Will you keep to the old way which wicked men have trod, who were cut down before their time, whose foundations were swept away by a flood? They said to God, "Depart from us! What can the Almighty do to them?"' (Job 22:15-17). There were therefore only eight persons who escaped the wrath of God, in the day that the flood came upon the earth; the rest were ungodly. There was also a world of them, and they are to this day in the prison of hell (Heb. 11:7; 1 Peter 3:19-20). No, I must correct my pen, there were but seven of the eight who were good; for Ham, though he escaped the judgement of the water, yet the curse of God overtook him to his damnation.

Second, when the world began again to be replenished and people began to multiply, how few, even in all ages, do we read of who were saved from the damnation of the world?

1. One Abraham and his wife, God called out of the land of the Chaldeans: 'Look to Abraham your father, and to Sarah who bore you; for I called him alone, and blessed him and increased him' (Isa. 51:2).

2. One Lot, out of Sodom and Gomorrah, out of Admah and Zeboiim; one Lot out of four cities! Indeed, his wife and two daughters went out of Sodom with him; but they all three proved to be nothing, as you may see in Genesis 19. For this reason, Peter observes that Lot only was saved: 'And turning the cities of Sodom and Gomorrah into ashes, condemned them to destruction, making them an example to those who afterwards would live ungodly; and delivered righteous Lot' (2 Peter 2:6-7). Jude says that in this condemnation, God overthrew, not only Sodom and Gomorrah, but the cities round about them also; and yet you find none but Lot could be found to be righteous, either in Sodom or Gomorrah, or the cities about them. For this reason, they, all of them, suffer the vengeance of eternal fire (Jude 7).

3. We come now to the time of the Judges. How few then were the godly, even then when the inhabitants of the villages ceased, they ceased in Israel! 'The highways [of God] were deserted' (Judg. 5:6).

4. There were but few in the days of David: 'Help, LORD, for the godly man ceases! For the faithful disappear from among the sons of men' (Ps. 12:1).

5. In Isaiah's time, the saved had come to such a few that he positively says that there were a very small number left: 'Unless the LORD of hosts had left to us a very small remnant, we would have become like Sodom, we would have been made like Gomorrah' (Isa. 1:9).

6. It was cried to them in the time of Jeremiah that they should 'run to and fro through the streets of Jerusalem; see now and know; and seek in her open places if you can find

a man, if there is anyone who executes judgement, who seeks the truth, and I will pardon her' (Jer. 5:1).

7. God showed his servant Ezekiel how few there would be saved in his day, by the vision of a few hairs saved out of the midst of a few hairs; for the saved were a few saved out of a few (Ezek. 5:1-5).

8. You find in the time of the prophet Micah, how the godly complain that, as to number, they were so few then, that he compares them to those who were left behind, when they had gathered the summer fruit (Micah 7:1).

9. When Christ came, how did he confirm this truth, that but few of those who put in a claim for heaven will have it for their inheritance? But the common people would not hear it, and therefore one time when he did but hint a little at this truth, the people, even all in the synagogue where he preached it 'were filled with wrath, and rose up and thrust him out of the city; and they led him to the brow of the hill on which their city was built, that they might throw him down over the cliff' (Luke 4:28-29).

10. John, who came after Christ, says, 'The whole world lies under the sway of the wicked one' (1 John 5:19), 'and all the world marvelled and followed the beast' (Rev. 13:3), 'and authority was given him over every tribe, tongue, and nation' (Rev. 13:7). Power to do what? Why, to cause all, both great and small, rich and poor, bond and free, to receive his mark, and to be branded for him.

11. Should we come to observation and experience, the display of the countenance of the bulk of men witnesses against them: 'They declare their sin as Sodom; they do not hide it' (Isa. 3:9). Where is the man who makes the Almighty God his delight and who desires his glory in the world? Do not even almost all pursue this world, their lusts and pleasures, and so, consequently, say to God, 'Depart from us, for

we desire not the knowledge of your ways'; or, 'What is the Almighty that we should serve him? It is in vain to serve God, etc.' So, without doubt, it will appear a truth in the Day of God that but few of those who shall put in their claim to heaven will have it for their inheritance.

Before I pass this section, I shall show you to what the saved are compared in the Scriptures.

1. They are compared to a handful: 'There shall be an handful of corn in the earth upon the top of the mountains' (Ps. 72:16, AV). This corn is nothing else but those who shall be saved (Matt. 3:12; 13:30). But note, 'There shall be an handful.' What is a handful, when compared with the whole heap? Or, what is a handful out of the rest of the world?

2. As they are compared to a handful, so are they compared to a lily among the thorns (S. of S. 2:2), which is rare and not so commonly seen: 'Like a lily among thorns,' says Christ, 'so is my love among the daughters.' By thorns, we understand the worst and best of men, even all who are destitute of the grace of God: 'The best of them is like a briar; the most upright is sharper than a thorn hedge' (Micah 7:4; 2 Sam. 23:6). I know that she may be called a lily among thorns also because she meets with the pricks of persecution (Ezek. 2:6; 28:24). She may also be thus termed to show the disparity that is between hypocrites and the church (Luke 8:14; Heb. 8). But this is not all. The saved are compared to a lily among thorns to show you that they are but few in the world; to show you that they are but few and rare; for as Christ compares her to a lily among thorns, so she compares him to an apple tree among the trees of the wood, which is rare and scarce, not common.

3. Those who are saved are called but one of many. For though there are sixty queens and eighty concubines and virgins without number, yet, 'My dove,' says Christ, 'my

perfect one, is the only one' (S. of S. 6:8-9); according to the words of Jeremiah, 'I will take you, one from a city' (3:14). The words of Paul are much like this: 'Do you not know that those who run in a race all run, but one receives the prize?' (1 Cor. 9:24). But one — that is, few of many, few of those who run; for he is not here comparing those who run with those who sit still, but with those who run. Some run and lose; some run and win. Those who run and win are few in comparison with those who run and lose: those who run in a race, all run, but one receives the prize. Let there then be sixty queens and eighty concubines and virgins without number, yet the saved are but few.

4. Those who are saved are compared to the gleaning after the vintage is in: 'Woe is me! For I am like those who gather summer fruits, like those who glean vintage grapes' (Micah 7:1). The gleanings! What are the gleanings to the whole crop? And, yet, you see here that the saved are compared to the gleanings. It is the devil and sin that carry away the cartloads, while Christ and his ministers come after a-gleaning: 'Is not the gleaning of the grapes of Ephraim better than the vintage of Abiezer?' (Judg. 8:2). Those who Christ and his ministers glean and bind up in the bundle of life are better than the loads that go the other way. You know it is often the cry of the poor in the harvest, 'Poor gleaning! Poor gleaning!' And the ministers of the gospel also cry, 'Who has believed our report? And to whom has the arm of the LORD been revealed?' (Isa. 53:1). When the prophet speaks of the saved using this same metaphor of gleaning, how does he amplify the matter? ' " Yet gleaning grapes will be left in it, like the shaking of an olive tree, two or three olives at the top of the uppermost bough, four or five in its most fruitful branches," says the LORD God of Israel' (Isa. 17:6). Thus you see what gleaning is left in the vineyard, after the vintage is in: two or three here, four or

five there. Alas, those who shall be saved when the devil
and hell have had their due will be but as the gleaning;
they will be but few. Those who go to hell, go there in
clusters, but the saved go not so to heaven (Matt. 13:30;
Micah 7). For this reason, when the prophet speaks of the
saved, he says, 'There is no cluster'; but when he speaks of
the damned, he says, 'They are gathered by clusters' (Rev.
14:18-19). O sinners, but few will be saved! O professing
believers, but few will be saved!

5. Those who shall be saved are compared to jewels:
'"They shall be mine," says the LORD of hosts, "on the day
that I make them my jewels"' (Mal. 3:17). Jewels, you know,
are rare things, things that are not found in every house.
Jewels will lie in a little space, being few and small, though
lumber takes up much. In almost every house you may find
brass and iron and lead; and, in every place you may find
hypocrites who claim to be believers. But the saved are not
these common things; they are God's peculiar treasure (Ps.
135:4). For this reason, Paul distinguishes between the
lumber and the treasure in the house: 'In a great house,' he
says, 'there are not only vessels of gold and silver, but also
of wood and clay, some for honour, and some for dishonour'
(2 Tim. 2:20). Here is a word for wooden and earthy professing believers: the jewels and treasure are vessels to honour,
those of wood and earth are vessels of dishonour — that is,
vessels for destruction (Rom. 9:21).

6. Those who shall be saved are compared to a remnant:
'Unless the LORD of hosts had left to us a very small remnant, we would have become like Sodom, we would have
been made like Gomorrah' (Isa. 1:9) — remnant, a small
remnant, a very small remnant! Oh, how the Holy Spirit
words it! And, all to show you how few shall be saved.
Everyone knows what a remnant is, but this is a small remnant, a very small remnant. So again, 'For thus says the

LORD: "Sing with gladness for Jacob, and shout among the chief of the nations; proclaim, give praise, and say, 'O LORD, save your people, the remnant of Israel!'"' (Jer. 31:7).

What shall I say? The saved are often in scripture called a remnant (Ezek. 9:4,8; Isa. 10:20-22; 11:11,16; Jer. 23:3; Joel 2:32). But what is a remnant to the whole piece? What is a remnant of people to the whole kingdom? Or, what is a remnant of wheat to the whole harvest?

7. The saved are compared to the tithe or tenth part. For this reason, when God sends the prophet to make the hearts of the people dull, their ears heavy, and to shut their eyes, the prophet asks, 'How long?' To this God answers, 'Until the cities are laid waste and without inhabitant, the houses are without a man, the land is utterly desolate, the LORD has removed men far away, and the forsaken places are many in the midst of the land.' (Isa. 6:11). 'But, yet,' as God says in another verse, 'a tenth will be in it, and will return and be for consuming, as a terebinth tree or as an oak, whose stump remains when it is cut down. So the holy seed shall be its stump' (Isa. 6:10-13). But what is a tenth? What is one in ten? And, yet, so speaks the Holy Spirit when he speaks of the holy seed, of those who were to be preserved from the judgement. And observe it, the fattening and blinding of the rest were to their everlasting destruction; and so, both Christ and Paul expound it often in the New Testament (Matt. 13:14-15; Mark 4:12; Luke 8:10; John 12:40; Acts 28:26; Rom. 11:8). So those who are reserved from those who perish will be very few — one in ten: 'A tenth shall return, so the holy seed shall be the substance thereof.'

I shall not add more general proof at this time. May God grant it that the world is not offended at these. But, without doubt, but few of those who shall put in their claim for heaven will have it for their inheritance, which will be seen further in the reading of that which follows. Therefore, I come more particularly to show you that but few will be saved. I say, but few professing believers themselves will be saved; for that is the truth that the text does more directly look at and defend. Therefore, give me your hand, good reader, and let us walk soberly through the rest of what shall be said; and let us compare, as we go, each detail with the holy Scripture.

1. It is said, 'So the daughter of Zion is left as a booth in a vineyard, as a hut in a garden of cucumbers, as a besieged city' (Isa. 1:8). The vineyard was the church of Israel (Isa. 5:1); the booth in that vineyard was the daughter of Zion, or the truly gracious among, or in that church. A booth — God had but a booth there, but a little habitation in the church, a very few who were truly gracious among the great multitude that professed faith. And, had it not been for these, for this booth, the rest would had been ruined like Sodom: 'Unless the Lord of Sabaoth had left us a seed [in the church], we would have become like Sodom, and we would have been made like Gomorrah' (Rom. 9:29). For this reason, among the multitude of those who shall be damned, those who profess faith will make a considerable party.

2. 'For though your people, O Israel, be as the sand of the sea, a remnant of them will return' (Isa. 10:22; Rom. 9:27). For though your people Israel, whom you brought out of Egypt, to whom you have given church-constitution, holy laws, holy ordinances, holy prophets, and holy covenants; your people by separation from all people, and your people by profession; though this your people be as the sand of the sea, a remnant shall be saved. For this reason, among the multitude of those who shall be damned, those who profess faith will make a considerable party.

3. 'People will call them rejected silver, because the Lord has rejected them' (Jer. 6:30). The people under

consideration here in Jeremiah 6:27 are called God's people, his people by profession: 'I have set you as an assayer and a fortress among my people, that you may know and test their way.' What follows? They are all grievous revolters, walking with slanderers, reprobate silver; the Lord has rejected them. In Jeremiah 7:29, they are also called the generation of his wrath: 'For the LORD has rejected and forsaken the generation of his wrath.' I gather this out of these holy Scriptures: that with reference to their profession and church constitution, a people may be called the people of God; but with reference to the event and final conclusion that God will make with some of them, they may be truly the generation of his wrath.

4. In Isaiah chapter 5, you read again of the vineyard of God, and that it was planted on a very fruitful hill, planted with the choicest vines, had a wall, a tower, a winepress belonging to it, and all things that could put it into right order and good government, as a church. But this vineyard of the Lord of hosts brought forth wild grapes, fruits unbecoming her constitution and government. For this reason, the Lord takes his hedge and wall from her, and lets her be trodden down. Read Christ's exposition on it in Matthew 21:33, etc. Look to it, those of you who make a profession [of faith], these are the words of the text, 'For many, I say to you, will seek to enter and will not be able' (Luke 13:24).

5. 'Son of man,' said God to the prophet, 'the house of Israel has become dross to me; they are all bronze, tin, iron and lead, in the midst of a furnace; they have become dross from silver' (Ezek. 22:18). God had silver there, some silver, but it was but little; the bulk of that people was but the dross of the church, though they were the members of it. But what does he mean by the dross? Why, he looked upon them as no better than the rabble of the world — that is, with respect to their latter end, notwithstanding their

church membership. For to be called dross is to be put among the rest of the sinners of the world in the judgement of God, though at present they abide in his house: 'You put away all the wicked of the earth like dross; therefore I love your testimonies.' (Ps. 119:119). God says of his saved ones, 'He has chosen [them] in the furnace of affliction' (Isa. 48:10, AV). The refiner, when he puts the silver into his furnace puts lead also among it. Now this lead being ordered as he knows how, works up the dross from the silver, which dross, still as it rises, he puts to the side, or takes away with an instrument. And thus God deals with his church. There is silver in his church, yes, and there is also dross. Now the dross are the hypocrites and graceless ones who have got into the church, and these will God reveal, and afterwards put away as dross. So that it will, without doubt, prove a truth of God that many of those who profess to be believers and who shall put in a claim for heaven will not have it for their inheritance.

6. It is said of Christ, 'His winnowing fan is in his hand, and he will thoroughly clean out his threshing floor, and gather his wheat into the barn; but he will burn up the chaff with unquenchable fire' (Matt. 3:12). The floor is the church of God: 'Oh, my threshing and the grain of my floor!' said God by the prophet to his people (Isa. 21:10). The wheat are those good ones in his church, who shall be undoubtedly saved; therefore, he says, 'Gather my wheat into my garner.' The chaff grows upon the same stalk and ear, and so it is in the same visible body with the wheat, but there is not substance in it. For this reason, in time they must be severed one from the other: the wheat must be gathered into the garner, which is heaven; and the chaff, or professing believers who lack true grace, must be gathered into hell, that they may be burned up with unquenchable fire. Therefore, let those who make a profession of faith consider it seriously.

7. Christ Jesus casts away two of the three grounds that are said to receive the Word (Luke 8:11-15). The stony ground received it with joy and the thorny ground brought forth fruit almost to perfection. Indeed, the highway ground was to show us that the carnal, whilst such, receive not the Word at all. But here is the pinch, two of the three who received it fell short of the kingdom of heaven; for but one of the three received it so as to bring forth fruit to perfection. Consider it seriously, professing believer.

8. The parable of the unprofitable servant (Matt. 25:24,29), the parable of the man without a wedding garment (Matt. 22:11-13), and the parable of the unsavoury salt (Matt. 5:13), each of them justifies this for truth . The parable of the unprofitable servant is to show us the sloth and idleness of some professing believers; that of the man without a wedding garment is to show us how some professing believers have the shame of their wickedness seen by God, even when they are among the children of the bridegroom; and that parable of the unsavoury salt is to show that as the salt that has lost its savour is fit for nothing, no, not for the dunghill, but to be trodden under a man's foot, so some professing believers — yes, and great ones, too, for this parable reached even one of the apostles — will in God's day be counted fit for nothing, but to be trodden down as the mire in the streets. Oh, the slothful, the naked, and unsavoury professing believer! How will they be rejected of God and his Christ in the Judgement! Consider this seriously, you who profess to be believers.

9. The parable of the tares also gives countenance to this truth. For though it is said that the field is the world, yet, it is said that the tares were sown even in the church: 'But while men slept, his enemy came and sowed tares among the wheat and went his way' (Matt. 13:24-25).

*Objection*:
But some may object, by saying that the tares might be sown in the world among the wheat, though not in the churches.
*Answer*:
But Christ, by expounding this parable, tells us that the tares were sown in his kingdom, the tares — that is, the children of the devil (Matt. 13:30,39). As therefore the tares are gathered and burned in the fire, so shall it be at the end of this world: 'The Son of Man will send out his angels, and they will gather out of his kingdom all things that offend, and those who practise lawlessness, and will cast them into the furnace of fire. There will be wailing and gnashing of teeth' (Matt. 13:41-42). Consider it seriously, you who profess faith.

10. The parable of the ten virgins also suits our purpose. These ten are called the kingdom of heaven (Matt. 25:1) — that is, the church of Christ, the visible rightly-constituted church of Christ; for they all went out of the world, all had lamps, and all went forth to meet the bridegroom. Yet, behold, what an overthrow the one-half of them met with at the gate of heaven: they were shut out, bid to depart, and Christ told them he did not know them (v. 10- 11). Tremble, you who profess faith! Pray, professing believer!

11. The parable of the net that was cast into the sea (Matt. 13:47-50) also countenances this truth. The substance of that parable is to show that souls may be gathered by the gospel, which is there compared to a net, may be kept in that net, drawn to a shore (to the world's end) by that net, and yet, may then prove to be bad fishes, and be cast away. The parable runs thus: 'Again, the kingdom of heaven [the gospel] is like a dragnet that was cast into the sea [the world] and gathered some of every kind [good and bad], which,

when it was full, they drew to shore [to the end of the world]; and they sat down [in judgement] and gathered the good into vessels, but threw the bad away.' Some bad fish, no, I doubt, a great many will be found in the net of the gospel at the Day of Judgement. Watch and be sober, you who profess to be believers.

12. 'And I say to you that many will come from east and west, and sit down with Abraham, Isaac, and Jacob in the kingdom of heaven. But the sons of the kingdom will be cast out' (Matt. 8:11-12). The children of the kingdom were those whose privileges were said to be these: 'To whom pertain the adoption, the glory, the covenants, the giving of the law, the service of God, and the promises' (Rom. 9:4). I take the liberty to refer all the more to the first church because that which happened to them, happened as types and examples, intimating that there is ground to think that things of as dreadful a nature are to happen among the churches of the Gentiles (1 Cor. 10:11-12.) Neither indeed have the Gentile churches security from God that as dreadful things shall not happen to them. And concerning this very thing, sufficient caution is given to us also (1 Cor. 6:9-10; Gal. 5:19-21; Eph. 5:3-7; Phil. 3:17-19; 2 Thess. 2:11-12; 2 Tim. 2:20-21; Heb. 6:4-9; Heb. 10:26-28; 2 Peter 2 - 3; 1 John 5:10; Rev. 2:20-22).

13. The parable of the true vine and its branches confirms what I have said (John 15:1-6). The vine there I understand to mean Christ, Christ as head; by the branches, I understand his church. Some of these branches proved fruitless castaways, were in time cast out of the church, were gathered by men and burned.

14. Lastly, I will come to specific instances. (1) The twelve had a devil among them (John 6:70). (2) Ananias and Sapphira were in the church of Jerusalem (Acts 5). (3) Simon

Magus was among the believers at Samaria (Acts 8). (4) Among the church of Corinth were those who had not the knowledge of God (1 Cor. 15:34). (5) Paul tells the Galatians that false brethren had crept in unawares (Gal. 2:4); and so does the apostle Jude (vv. 3-4), and yet they were as quick-sighted to see as any nowadays. (6) The church in Sardis had but a few names in her, to whom the kingdom of heaven belonged: 'You have a few names even in Sardis who have not defiled their garments; and they shall walk with me in white, for they are worthy' (Rev. 3:4). (7) As for the church of the Laodiceans, it is called 'wretched, miserable, poor, blind, and naked' (Rev. 3:17). So put all things together, and I may boldly say, as I also have said already, that among the multitude of those who shall be damned, those who profess to be believers will make a considerable party. Or, to express it in the words of the observation: when men have put in all the claim they can for heaven, but few will have it for their inheritance.

I will now show you some reasons of the point, besides those five that I showed you before. But, first, I will show you why the poor, carnal, ignorant world miss of heaven, and then, second, why knowledgeable professing believers miss of it also.

1. The poor, carnal, ignorant world miss of heaven because they love their sins and cannot part with them: 'Men loved darkness rather than light, because their deeds were evil' (John 3:19). The poor, ignorant world miss of heaven because they are enemies in their minds to God, his Word, and holiness: they must be all damned who take pleasure in unrighteousness (2 Thess. 2:10-12). The poor, ignorant world miss of heaven because they stop their ears against convictions, and refuse to come when God calls:

Because I have called and you refused,
I have stretched out my hand and no one regarded,
Because you disdained all my counsel,
And would have none of my rebuke,
I also will laugh at your calamity;
I will mock when your terror comes,
When your terror comes like a storm,
And your destruction comes like a whirlwind,
When distress and anguish come upon you.
Then they will call on me, but I will not answer;
They will seek me diligently, but they will not
    find me.
Because they hated knowledge
And did not choose the fear of the LORD'
                              (Prov. 1:24-29).

2. The poor, ignorant world miss of heaven because the god of this world has blinded their eyes, so that they can neither see the evil and damnable state they are in at present, nor the way to get out of it; neither do they see the beauty of Jesus Christ, nor how willing he is to save poor sinners (2 Cor. 4:3-4).

3. The poor, ignorant world miss of heaven because they put off and defer coming to Christ, until the time of God's patience and grace has passed. Some indeed are resolved never to come; but some again say, 'We will come here-after'; and so it comes to pass, that because God called and they did not hear, '"So they called out and I would not listen," says the LORD of hosts' (Zech. 7:11-13).

4. The poor, ignorant world miss of heaven because they have false apprehensions of God's mercy. They say in their hearts, 'We shall have peace, though we walk in the

imagination of our heart, to add drunkenness to thirst.' But what says the Word? 'The LORD would not spare him; for then the anger of the LORD and his jealousy would burn against that man, and every curse that is written in this book would settle on him, and the LORD would blot out his name from under heaven' (Deut. 29:20).

5. The poor, ignorant world miss of heaven because they make light of the gospel that offers mercy to them freely, and because they lean upon their own good thinking, and reasonings, and doings (Matt. 22:1-6; Rom. 9:30-32).

6. The poor, carnal world miss of heaven because by unbelief, which reigns in them, they are kept for ever from being clothed with Christ's righteousness and from washing in his blood, without which there is neither remission of sin nor justification.

But to pass these till shortly I come, in the next place, to show you some reasons why the person who professes faith falls short of heaven.

First, in general, they rest in things lower than special grace, such as in awakenings that are not special, in repentance that is not special, etc.; and they rest a little in running a parallel between the one and the other, that, if God will, they may see and escape.

1. Have those who shall be saved awakenings about their state by nature? So have those who shall be damned. Those who never go to heaven may see much of sin and of the wrath of God which it is due. This had Cain and Judas, and yet they came short of the kingdom (Gen. 4; Matt. 27:4). The saved have convictions, leading to eternal life; but the others convictions are not so. The convictions of the one drive them sincerely to Christ; the convictions of the other drive them to the law, and the law, finally, to desperation.

2. There is a repentance that will not save, a repentance to be repented of; and a repentance to salvation, not to be repented of (2 Cor. 7:10). Yet, so great a similarity and likeness is there between the one and the other, that most times the wrong is taken for the right, and through this mistake those who profess to be believers perish. As,

1. In saving repentance there will be an acknowledgement of sin; and one that has the other repentance may acknowledge his sins also (Matt. 27:4).

2. In saving repentance there is a crying out under sin; but one who has the other repentance may cry out under sin also (Gen. 4:13).

3. In saving repentance there will be humiliation for sin; and one that has the other repentance may humble himself also (1 Kings 21:29).

4. Saving repentance is accompanied by self-loathing; but he that has the other repentance may have loathing of sin too (2 Peter 2:22). A loathing of sin because it is sin, that he cannot have; but a loathing of sin because it is offensive to him, that he may have. The dog does not loathe that which troubles his stomach because it is there, but because it troubles him. When it no longer troubles him, he can turn to it again, and lick it up just as he did before it troubled him.

5. Saving repentance is accompanied by prayers and tears; but he who has none but the other repentance may have prayers and tears also (Gen. 27:34-35; Heb. 12:14-16).

6. In saving repentance, there is fear and reverence for the Word and the ministers that bring it; but this may also be so where there is none but the repentance that is not saving. For Herod feared John, knowing that he was a just and holy man, and observed him; when he heard him, he did many things, and heard him gladly (Mark 6:20).

7. Saving repentance makes a man's heart very tender of doing anything against the Word of God. But Balaam could say, 'If Balak were to give me his house full of silver and gold, I could not go beyond the Word of the LORD' (Num. 24:13).

See, then, how far a man may go in repentance, and yet be short of that which is called 'Repentance to salvation, not to be repented of.' (1) He may be awakened; (2) he may acknowledge his sin; (3) he may cry out under the burden of sin; (4) he may have humility for it; (5) he may loathe it; (6) may have prayers and tears against it; (7) may delight to do many things of God; (8) may be afraid of sinning against him; and after all this, may perish for the lack of saving repentance.

Second, do those who shall be saved have faith? Why, those who shall not be saved may have faith also; yes, a faith in many things so like the faith that saves that they can hardly be distinguished — though they differ both in root and branch. To come to particulars:

1. Saving faith has Christ for its object, and so also may the faith that is not saving faith. Those very Jews of whom it is said that they believed on Christ, Christ tells them, and that after their believing in him, 'You are of your father the devil, and the desires of your father you want to do' (John 8:44).

2. Saving faith is wrought by the Word of God, and so may the faith that is not saving (Luke 8:13).

3. Saving faith looks for justification without works, and so may a faith that is not saving.

4. Saving faith will sanctify and purify the heart, and the faith that is not saving may discourage a man from the pollutions of the world, as it did Judas, Demas, and others (See 2 Peter 2).

5. Saving faith will give a man tastes of the world to come, and also joy by those tastes, and so will the faith that is not saving (Heb. 6:4-5; Luke 8:13).

6. Saving faith will help a man, if he is called to it, to give his body to be burned for his religion, and so will the faith that is not saving (1 Cor. 13:1-5).

7. Saving faith will help a man to look for an inheritance in the world to come, and so may the faith that is not saving: 'Ten virgins took their lamps and went out to meet the bridegroom' (Matt. 25:1).

8. Saving faith will not only make a man look for, but prepare to meet the bridegroom, and so may the faith that is not saving: 'Then all those virgins arose and trimmed their lamps' (Matt. 25:7).

9. Saving faith will make a man look for an interest in the kingdom of heaven with confidence, and the faith that is not saving will even demand entrance of the Lord: 'Lord, Lord, open to us!' (Matt. 25:11).

10. Saving faith will have good works follow it into heaven, and the faith that is not saving may have great works follow it as far as heaven's gates: 'Lord, Lord, have we not prophesied in your name, cast out demons in your name, and done many wonders in your name?' (Matt. 7:22).

Now, then, if the faith that is not saving may have Christ for its object, be brought into being by the Word, look for justification without works, discourage men from the pollutions of the world, and give men tastes of, and joy in, the things of another world, I say, again, if it will help a man to burn for his judgement, and to look for an inheritance in another world; yes, if it will help a man to prepare for it, claim interest in it, and if it can carry great works — many great and glorious works as far as heaven's gates — then it is no marvel if an abundance of people take this

faith for *the* saving faith, and so fall short of heaven by it.
Alas, friends, there are but few who can produce such for
repentance; and such faith, as you see I have proved, even
reprobates have had in several ages of the church!

But, third, those who go to heaven are a praying people;
but a man may pray who shall not be saved. Pray! He may
pray, pray daily; yes, he may ask of God the ordinances of
justice (Isa. 28:2), and may take delight in approaching God.
No, further, such souls may, as it were, cover the altar of
the Lord with tears, with weeping and crying out (Mal. 2:13).

Fourth, do God's people keep holy fasts? Those who are
not his people may keep fasts also — may keep fasts often,
even twice a week: 'The Pharisee stood and prayed thus
with himself, "God, I thank you that I am not like other
men — extortioners, unjust, adulterers, or even as this tax
collector. I fast twice a week; I give tithes of all that I possess"' (Luke 18:11-12). I might go into greater depth about
things, but I intend to write just a little book. I do not question it that many Balaamites will appear before the judgement seat to condemnation: men who have had visions of
God (Num. 24:2) and who have had the knowledge of the
Most High (vv. 4,16); men who have had the Spirit of God
come upon them and who have by that been turned into
other men (1 Sam. 10:6,10). Yet, these shall go to the gener-
ations of their fathers; they shall never see light (Ps. 49:19).

I read of some men whose excellency in religion mounts
up to heavens and their heads reach to the clouds, who yet
shall perish for ever like their own refuse; and he who has
seen them in this world, shall say at the judgement, 'Where
are they?' (Job 20:5-7). There will be many who were gal-
lant in their profession [of faith] in this world, who will be
missing from among the saved in the day of Christ's coming.
Yes, many whose damnation was never dreamed of. Which
of the twelve ever thought that Judas would have proved to

be a devil? No, when Christ suggested that one among them was nothing, they each were more afraid of themselves than of him (Matt. 26:21-23). Who questioned the salvation of the foolish virgins? The wise ones did not; they gave them the privilege of communion with them (Matt. 25:1-13). The discerning of the heart and the infallible proof of the truth of saving grace are reserved for the judgement of Jesus Christ at his coming. The church and the best of saints sometimes hit and sometimes miss in their judgements about this matter. And the cause of our missing in our judgement is:

1. Partly because we cannot infallibly, at all times, distinguish grace that saves from that which only appears to do so;

2. Partly also because some men are skilled in giving right names to wrong things;

3. And partly because, we being commanded to receive him who is weak, are afraid to exclude the least Christian. By hidden means hypocrites creep into the churches. But what says the scripture? 'I, the Lord, search the heart, I test the mind,' (Jer. 17:10; also 11:20), and again, 'All the churches shall know that I am he who searches the minds and hearts. And I will give to each one of you according to your works' (Rev. 2:23). To this searcher of hearts is the time of infallible discerning reserved; and then you shall see how far grace that is not saving has gone, and also how few will be saved indeed. May the Lord awaken poor sinners by my little book!

# *III*

## Use and application

I come now to make some brief use and application of the whole; and my first word shall be to the openly profane.

Poor sinner, you read here that but a few will be saved, that many who expect to gain heaven will go without heaven. What do you say to this, poor sinner? Let me say it over again. There are but few to be saved, but very few. Let me add, but few of those who make a profession of faith, but few eminent professing believers. What do you say now, sinner? If judgement begins at the house of God, what will the end of those be who obey not the gospel of God? This is Peter's question. Can you answer it, sinner? Yes, I say again, if judgement must begin with them, will it not make you think, 'What shall become of me?' And I add, when you shall see the stars of heaven tumbling down to hell, can you think that such a muck-heap of sin as you are shall be lifted up to heaven? Peter asks you another question, namely, 'If the righteous one is scarcely saved, where will the ungodly and the sinner appear?' (1 Peter 4:18). Can you answer this question, sinner? Stand among the righteous you may not: 'Therefore the ungodly shall not stand in the judgement, nor sinners in the congregation of the righteous' (Ps. 1:5). Stand among the wicked, you then will not dare to do.

Where will you appear, sinner? To stand among the hypocrites will avail you nothing: 'For a hypocrite could not come before him' (Job 13:16) — that is, with acceptance, but shall perish. Because it concerns you much, let me go over it with you again. When you shall see lesser sinners than you are, bound up by angels in bundles, to burn them, where will you appear, sinner? You may wish yourself to be another man, but that will not help you, sinner. You may wish, 'If only I had been converted in time!', but that will not help you either. And if, like the wife of Jeroboam, you should pretend to be another woman, the Prophet, the Lord Jesus, would soon find you out! (1 Kings 14:2,5-6). What will you do, poor sinner? Heavy tidings, heavy tidings will come upon you, except you repent, poor sinner! (Luke 13:3,5). Oh, the dreadful state of a poor sinner, of an openly profane sinner! Everybody who has but common sense knows that this man is in the broad way to death, yet he laughs at his own damnation. Shall I mention particular references to you?

1. Poor, unclean sinner, the harlot's house is the way to hell, going down to the chambers of death (Prov. 2:18; 5:5; 7:27).

2. Poor, swearing and thievish sinner, God has prepared the curse, that every one who steals shall be cut off, as on this side, according to it; and every one who swears shall be cut off on that side, according to it (Zech. 5:3).

3. Poor, drunken sinner, what shall I say to you? 'Woe … to the drunkards of Ephraim' (Isa. 28:1); 'Woe to men mighty at drinking wine, woe to men valiant for mixing intoxicating drink' (Isa. 5:22); 'The unrighteous will not inherit the kingdom of God' (1 Cor. 6:9-10).

4. Poor, covetous worldly man, God's Word says that the covetous the Lord abhors; that the covetous man is an

idolator; and that the covetous shall not inherit the kingdom of God (Ps. 10:3; John 2:15; Eph. 5:5; 1 Cor. 6:9-10).

5. And you, liar, what will you do? 'All liars shall have
their part in the lake which burns with fire and brimstone,
which is the second death' (Rev. 21:8,27). I shall not enlarge upon it. Poor sinner, let no man deceive you: 'For because of these things the wrath of God comes upon the sons
of disobedience' (Eph. 5:6). I will therefore give you a brief
call and then leave you.

Sinner, awake! Yes, I say to you, 'Awake! Sin lies at your
door, and God's axe lies at your root, and hell-fire is right
underneath you!' I say, again, 'Awake!' (Gen.3:10). 'Therefore every tree which does not bear good fruit is cut down
and thrown into the fire' (Matt. 3:10).

Poor sinner, awake! Eternity and his Son are coming;
they are both coming to judge the world! Awake! Are you
still asleep, poor sinner? Let me place the trumpet at your
ear once again. The heavens will shortly be a burning flame;
the earth, and its works, shall be burned up, and then
wicked men shall go into ruin. Do you hear this, sinner?
(2 Peter 3). Hark, again, the sweet morsels of sins will then
be fled and gone, and the bitter burning fruits of them only
left. What say you now, sinner? Can you drink hell-fire?
Will the wrath of God be a pleasant dish to your taste? This
must be your meat and drink every day in hell, sinner. I
will still propound to you God's ponderous question, and
then for this time leave you: 'Can your heart endure, or can
your hands remain strong, in the days when I shall deal
with you?' says the Lord (Ezek. 22:14). What say you? Will
you answer this question now? Or, will you take time to do
it? Or, will you be desperate and risk all? And let me put
this text in your ear to keep it open: 'Upon the wicked he
will rain coals; fire and brimstone and a burning wind shall

be the portion of their cup' (Ps. 11:6); and so may the Lord have mercy upon you. Repent, sinners!

Second, my second word is to those who are upon the potter's wheel, concerning whom we know not as yet whether their convictions and awakenings will end in conversion or not. Several things I shall say to you, both to further your convictions and to caution you from staying anywhere below, or short of, saving grace.

1. Remember that but few shall be saved; and if God should count you worthy to be one of those few, what mercy would that be!

2. Be thankful therefore for convictions. Conversion begins at conviction, though all conviction does not end in conversion. It is a great mercy to be convinced that we are sinners and that we need a Saviour. Count it therefore a mercy. And that your convictions may end in conversion, take heed not to stifle them. It is the way of poor sinners to look upon convictions as things that are hurtful; and therefore they usually shun the awakening ministry and check a convicting conscience. Such poor sinners are much like the unruly boy who stands at the maid's elbow, to blow out her candle as fast as she lights it at the fire. Convinced sinner, God lights your candle, and you put it out; God lights it again, and you put it out: 'How oft is the candle of the wicked put out?' (Job 21:17, AV). Finally, God resolves that he will light your candle no more; and then, like Egyptians, you will dwell all your days in darkness, and never see light more, but by the light of hell-fire. For this reason, give glory to God, and if he awakens your conscience, quench not your convictions: 'Give glory to the LORD your God before he causes darkness, and before your feet stumble on the dark mountains, and while you are looking for light,

he turns it into the shadow of death and makes it dense darkness' (Jer. 13:16).

1. Be willing to see the worst of your condition. It is better to see it here than in hell; for you must see your misery here or there.

2. Beware of little sins. They will make way for great ones, and they again will make way for bigger ones, upon which God's wrath will follow; and then your latter end may be worse than your beginning (2 Peter 2:20).

3. Take heed of bad company and evil communication, for that will corrupt good manners. God says that evil company will turn you away from following him and will tempt you to serve other gods, demons: 'So the anger of the LORD will be aroused against you and destroy you suddenly' (Deut. 7:4).

4. Beware of such thoughts which bid you delay repentance, for that is damnable (Prov. 1:24; Zech. 7:12-13).

5. Beware of taking example from some poor, carnal person who professes to be a believer, whose religion lies on the tip of his tongue. Beware, I say, of the man whose head swims with notions, but his life is among the unclean (Job 36:14). 'He who walks with wise men will be wise, but the companion of fools will be destroyed' (Prov. 13:20).

6. Give yourself much to the Word, and prayer, and good discussion.

7. Labour to see the sin that cleaves to the best of your performances, and know that all is nothing if you are not found in Jesus Christ.

8. Keep in remembrance that God's eye is upon your heart and upon all your ways: '"Can anyone hide himself in secret places, so I shall not see him?" says the LORD; "Do I not fill heaven and earth?" says the LORD' (Jer. 23:24).

9. Be often meditating upon death and judgement (Eccles. 11:9; 12:14).

10. Be often thinking what a dreadful end sinners who have neglected Christ will have at that day of death and judgement (Heb. 10:31).

11. In your thoughts, put yourself often before Christ's judgement seat, in your sins, and consider with yourself, 'Were I now before my Judge, how would I look! How would I shake and tremble!'

12. Be often thinking of those who are now in hell past all mercy. I say, be often thinking of them thus:

1. They were once in the world, as I now am.
2. They once took delight in sin, as I have done.
3. They once neglected repentance, as Satan would have me do.
4. But now they are gone; now they are in hell; now the pit has shut her mouth upon them.

You may also double your thoughts of the damned thus:

1. If these poor people were in the world again, would they sin as they did before? Would they neglect salvation as they did before?
2. If they had sermons, as I have; if they had the Bible, as I have; if they had good company, as I have; yes, if they had a day of grace, as I have; would they neglect it as they did before? Sinner, if you could think soberly of these things, they might help — God blessing them — to awaken you and to keep you awakened until you reach repentance, the repentance that is to salvation, never to be repented of.

*Objection*:

But you have said few shall be saved, and some who go a great way are not saved. At this therefore I am even discouraged and disheartened. I think I had as good go no further. I am indeed under conviction, but I may perish; and if I go on in my sins, I can only perish; and it is ten, twenty, or a hundred to one if I am saved, though I am ever so earnest for heaven.

*Answer*:

That few will be saved is most certainly a truth, for Christ has said it; that many go far and come short of heaven, is as true, being testified by the same hand.

'But what then? Why, then, I had as good as never seek it!'

'Who told you so? Must nobody seek because few are saved? This is quite contrary to the text that bids us strive for it: "Strive to enter" because the gate is narrow, and because many will seek to enter in and shall not be able. But why go back again, seeing that is the nearest way to hell? Never go over hedge and ditch to hell.'

'If I must go there, I will go the furthest way round.'

'But who can tell, though there should not be so many saved as their shall, but you may be one of that few?'

Those who miss of life perish because they will not let go their sins, or because they take up a profession of faith which is short of the saving faith of the gospel. They perish, I say, because they are content with such things that will not prove graces of a saving nature when they come to be tried in the fire. Otherwise, the promise is free, and full, and everlasting: 'The one who comes to me, I will by no means cast out' (John 6:37). 'For God so loved the world that he gave his only begotten son, that whoever believes in him, should not perish but have everlasting life' (John 3:16).

For this reason, let not this *few shall be saved* weaken your heart, though, but let it cause you to quicken your pace, to improve your cries, to consider well your grounds for heaven. Let it make you fly faster from sin to Christ; let it keep you awake, and out of carnal security, and you may be saved.

Third, my third word is to those who profess to have faith. Sirs, give me permission to set my trumpet to you ears again, a little. When every man has put in all the claim he can for heaven, but few will have it for their inheritance. I mean but few of those who profess faith, for such is the intention of the text, and so I have also proved: 'For many, I say to you, will seek to enter and will not be able.' Let me therefore discuss the matter earnestly a little with you. Oh, the thousands of you who profess faith!

1. I begin with you whose religion lies only in your tongues. I mean you who are little, or not known from the rest of the rabble of the world, apart from the fact that you can talk better than they. Hear a word or two from me. If I speak with the tongue of men and angels, and have not charity — that is, love to God, and Christ, and saints, and holiness, I am nothing — not a child of God, and so have nothing to do with heaven (1 Cor. 13:1-2). A talkative tongue will not unlock the gates of heaven, nor blind the eyes of the Judge. Consider this: 'The wise in heart will receive commands, but a prating fool will fall' ( Prov. 10:8).

2. Covetous professing believer, you who make a gain of religion, who use your profession [of faith] to bring corn to your mill, consider it also. Gain is not godliness. Judas's religion lay much in the bag, but his soul is now burning in hell. All covetousness is idolatry. But what is that, or what will you call it, when men are religious for filthy lucre's sake? (Ezek. 33:31).

3. Indulgent professing believers, I have a word for you. I mean you who can tell how to misuse Scripture to maintain

your pride, your banqueting and abominable idolatry. Read
what Peter says. You are the snare and damnation of others:
'They allure through the lusts of the flesh, through lewd-
ness, the ones who have actually escaped from those who
live in error' (2 Peter 2:18). Besides, the Holy Spirit has a
great deal against you for your feastings and eating without
fear, not for health, but gluttony (Jude 12).

Further, Peter says, 'Those who count it pleasure to ca-
rouse in the daytime ... are spots and blemishes, carousing
in their own deceptions while they feast with you' (2 Peter
2:13).

And let me ask, 'Did God give his Word to justify your
wickedness? Or does grace teach you to plead for the flesh,
or for making provision for the lusts thereof?' Of these also
are those who feed their bodies to strengthen their lusts,
under pretence of strengthening frail nature. But I beg you,
remember the text: 'Many, I say to you, will seek to enter
and will not be able.'

4. I come next to the opinionist. I mean to him whose
religion lies in some circumstantials of religion. With this
sort, this kingdom swarms in this day. These think that those
who are not of their mode are all out of the way, when they
themselves may be out of the way in the midst of their zeal
for their opinions. I beg you, too, observe the text: 'Many, I
say to you, will seek to enter and will not be able.'

5. Neither is the formalist exempted from this number.
He is a man who has lost all but the shell of religion. He is
hot indeed for his legalistic forms and no marvel, for that is
all he has to contend for. But his form being without the
power and spirit of godliness will leave him in his sins; no,
he stands now in them in the sight of God (2 Tim. 3:5), and is
one of the many that 'will seek to enter and will not be able'.

6. The legalist comes next, even he who has no life except
what he makes out of his duties. This man has chosen to

stand and fall by Moses, who is the one who condemns the world: 'There is one who accuses you — Moses, in whom you trust' (John 5:45).

7. There is, in the next place, the libertine — he who pretends to be against forms and duties, considering them things that engender bondage, neglecting the order of God. This man pretends to pray always, but under that pretence, prays not at all. He pretends to keep every day a Sabbath, but this pretence only serves to cause him to cast off all set times for the worship of God. This is also one of the many who 'will seek to enter and will not be able' (Titus 1:16).

8. There is the temporising Latitudinarian. He is a man who has no God but his belly, nor any religion but that by which his belly is worshipped. His religion is always, like the times, turning this way and that way, like the cock on the steeple. Neither has he any conscience but a benumbed and seared one, and is next door to a downright atheist. He is also one of the many who 'will seek to enter and will not be able'.

9. There is also the wilfully ignorant professor of faith, or he who is afraid to know more, for fear of the cross. He is for picking and choosing of truth, and loves not to hazard his all for that worthy name by which he would be called. At any time, when he is overcome by arguments or awakenings of conscience, he uses these words to heal all by: 'I was not brought up in this faith'; as if it were unlawful for Christians to know more than has been taught them at first conversion. There are many scriptures that stand against this man, as the mouths of great guns, and he is one of the many that 'will seek to enter and will not be able'.

10. We will add to all these the man who would prove himself a Christian by comparing himself with others, instead of comparing himself with the Word of God. This man comforts himself because he is as holy as such and such a

person. He also knows as much as that person who has professed faith for a long time, and then concludes he shall go to heaven — as if he knew for certain that those with whom he compares himself would undoubtedly be saved. But what if he should be mistaken? No, may they not both fall short? But to be sure, he is in the wrong who has made the comparison (2 Cor. 10:12); and a wrong foundation will not stand in the Day of Judgement. This man therefore is one of the many that 'will seek to enter and will not be able'.

11. There is yet another person who makes a profession of faith, and he is for God and for Baal too. He can be any thing for any company: he can throw stones with both hands; his religion alters as fast as his company; he is a frog of Egypt, and can live in the water and out of the water; he can live in religious company, and again as well out of it. Nothing that is disorderly comes amiss to him; he will hold with the hare and run with the hound; he carries fire in the one hand, and water in the other; he is a very any thing but what he should be. This is also one of the many that 'will seek to enter and will not be able'.

12. There is also that free-willer, who denies to the Holy Spirit the sole work in conversion; and that Socinian, who denies to Christ that he has made satisfaction for sin to God; and that Quaker, who takes from Christ the two natures in his person; and I might add as many more, concerning whose damnation (if they die as they are) the Scripture is plain. These 'will seek to enter and will not be able'.

But, fourth, if it is so, what a strange disappointment will many who profess faith meet with at the Day of Judgement! I speak not now to the openly profane. Everybody, as I have said, who has but common understanding between good and evil, knows that they are in the broad way to hell and damnation, and that they will also come there too. Nothing can prevent it but repentance to salvation, except God should prove to be a liar by saving them then, and it is hard risking of that.

Neither is it amiss, if we take notice of the examples that are briefly mentioned in the Scripture, concerning those who profess faith but who fall short.

1. Judas perished from among the apostles (Acts 1).

2. Demas, as I think, perished from among the evangelists (2 Tim. 4:10).

3. Diotrephes perished from among the ministers, or those in office in the church (3 John 9).

4. And, as for Christians who make a profession of faith, they have fallen by heaps, and almost by whole churches (2 Tim. 1:15; Rev. 3:4,15-17).

5. Let us add to these that the things mentioned in the Scripture about these matters are but brief hints anditems of what is to happen afterwards, as the apostle said, 'Some men's sins are clearly evident, preceding them to judgement, but those of some men follow later' (1 Tim. 5:24).

So, fellow professing believer, let us fear, lest a promise being left us of entering into this rest, any of us should seem to come short of it. Oh, to come short! Nothing kills like it; nothing will burn like it. I intend not discouragements, but awakenings. The churches have need of awakening, and so have all professing believers. Do not despise me therefore but hear me over again. What a strange disappointment will many professing believers meet with at the day of God Almighty? A disappointment, I say, and that as to several things:

1. They will look to escape hell, and yet fall just into the mouth of hell! What a disappointment will be in this!

2. They will look for heaven, but the gate of heaven will be shut against them! What a disappointment is in this!

3. They will expect that Christ should have compassion for them, but will find that he has shut up all bowels of compassion from them! What a disappointment is in this!

Again, fifth, as this disappointment will be fearful, so certainly it will be very full of shock and terror.

1. Will it not be shocking to them to be unexpectedly excluded from life and salvation?

2. Will it not be shocking to them to see their own madness and folly, while they consider how they have dallied with their own souls and taken lightly for granted that they had that grace that would save them, but has left them in a damnable state?

3. Will they not also be shocked one at another, while they remember how in their lifetime they counted themselves fellowheirs of life? To allude to the words of the prophet, 'They shall be amazed at one another; their faces will be like flames' (Isa. 13:8).

4. Will it not be shocking to some of the damned themselves, to see some come to hell whom they shall then see come there? [Will it not be shocking] to see preachers of the Word, those who profess to be of the Word, those who profess to be in the Word coming there? What wondering was there among them at the fall of the King of Babylon, since he thought he had swallowed up all, and because he was run down by the Medes and Persians! 'How are you fallen from heaven, O Lucifer, son of the morning! How you are cut down to the ground, you who weakened the nations!' If such a thing as this will with shock surprise the

damned, what a shock it will be to them to see such a one as he, whose head reached to the clouds, to see him come down to the pit and perish for ever, like his own dung! 'Hell from beneath is excited about you, to meet you at your coming; it stirs up the dead for you, all the chief ones of the earth; it has raised up from their thrones all the kings of the nations' (Isa. 14:9). Those who see you will gaze at you, and consider you saying, 'Is this the man? Is this the man who professed faith and disputed and forsook us? Is this he who separated from us? But now he is fallen with us into the same eternal damnation with us.'

Sixth, yet again, one word more, if I may awaken those who profess to have faith. Consider this: though the poor, carnal world shall certainly perish, yet they will lack these things to aggravate their sorrow, which you will meet with in every thought that you will have of the condition you were in when you were in the world.

1. They will not have a profession of faith to torment them when they come there.

2. They will not have a taste of a lost heaven to torment them when they come there.

3. They will not have the thoughts of 'I was almost at heaven' to torment them when they come there.

4. They will not have the thoughts of how they cheated saints, ministers and churches to torment them when they come there.

5. They will not have the dying thoughts of false faith, false hope, false repentance, and false holiness to torment them when they come there: 'I was at the gates of heaven; I looked into heaven; I thought I should have entered into heaven.' Oh, how these things will sting! They will, if I may call them so, be the sting of the sting of death in hell-fire.

Seventh, grant me now to give you, in a word, a little advice.

1. Do you love your own soul? Then pray to Jesus Christ for an awakened heart, for a heart so awakened with all the things of another world that you may be allured to Jesus Christ.

2. When you come there, beg again for more awakenings about sin, hell, grace, and about the righteousness of Christ.

3. Cry also for a spirit of discernment that you may know that which is saving grace indeed.

4. Above all studies, apply yourself to the study of those things that show you the evil of sin, the shortness of man's life, and which is the way to be saved.

5. Keep company with the most godly among those who profess faith.

6. When you hear what the nature of true grace is, defer not to ask your own heart if this grace is there. And here take heed: (1) that the preacher himself is sound and of good life; (2) that you take not apparent graces for real ones, nor apparent fruits for real fruits. (3) Take heed that a sin in your life goes not unrepented of; for that will make a flaw in your evidence, a wound in your conscience, and a breach in your peace; and a hundred to one, if at last it does not drive all the grace in you into so dark a corner of your heart that, for a time, you shall not be able, by all the torches that are burning in the gospel, to find it out to your own comfort and consolation.

# *Contents*

# The Heavenly Footman

'Run in such a way
that you may obtain it'
(1 Cor. 9:24).

# The Heavenly Footman

*Or a description of the man who gets to heaven, together with an explanation of how he travels, the signs he follows, and some directions on how to travel in such a way as to be granted entrance into heaven.*

So it came to pass, when they had brought them outside, that he said, 'Escape for your life! Do not look behind you nor stay anywhere in the plain. Escape to the mountains, lest you be destroyed' (Gen. 19:17).

## A letter to all slothful and careless people

Friends,

Solomon said, 'The desire of the lazy man kills him' (Prov. 21:25); and if so, what will slothfulness do to those who entertain it? The proverb is: 'He who sleeps in harvest is a son who causes shame' (Prov. 10:5); and dare I be bold enough to say this: no greater shame can befall a man than to see that he has fooled away his soul and sinned away eternal life. And I am sure this is the best way to do it, namely, to be slothful, slothful, I say, in the work of salvation. The vineyard of the slothful man, with reference to

the things of this life, has no more briars, nettles and stinking weeds than he who is slothful for heaven has his heart
full of heart-choking and soul-damning sin.

Slothfulness has these two evils: first, to neglect the time
it should be using to gain heaven, and thereby, in the second
place, resulting in untimely repentance. I can assure you
that he who loses his soul in this world through slothfulness will have no cause to be glad about it when he comes
to hell. Slothfulness is usually accompanied by carelessness, and carelessness is, for the most part, caused by senses
which are dulled to spiritual realities, and this, again, puts
renewed strength into slothfulness, and by this means the
soul is left without remedy. Slothfulness shuts out Christ;
slothfulness shames the soul (S. of S. 5:2-4; Prov. 13:4).

Slothfulness is condemned even by the feeblest of all
creatures: 'Go to the ant, you sluggard! Consider her ways
and be wise' (Prov. 6:6). 'The lazy man will not plough because of winter' — that is, he will not break up the fallow
ground of his heart, because there must be some effort made
by him who would do it. Therefore, 'he will beg during the
harvest' (Prov. 20:4) — that is, when the saints of God shall
have their glorious heaven and happiness given to them.
But the sluggard will 'have nothing' — that is, he will be
none the better for all his crying for mercy, according to
what is stated in Matthew 25:10-12.

If you would know who is a sluggard in the things of
heaven, compare him with one who is slothful in the things
of this world. (1) He who is slothful is loath to set about the
work he should pursue; and so is he who is slothful for
heaven. (2) He who is slothful is one who is willing to make
delays; and so is he who is slothful for heaven. (3) He who
is a sluggard uses any small obstacle as an excuse to put off
doing his work; and so is it with the man who is slothful
for heaven. (4) He who is slothful does his work by halves;

and so is it with the man who is slothful for heaven. He may almost, but shall never quite obtain complete deliverance from hell. He may almost, but shall never (unless he mends his ways) fully become a saint. (5) Those who are slothful usually miss the season in which things are to be done; and so it is with those who are slothful for heaven. They miss the season of grace. And therefore (6) those who are slothful seldom if ever produce good fruit; and so it will also be with the soul-sluggard. (7) Those who are slothful are rebuked for it. So will Christ deal with those who are not working for him. 'Out of your own mouth I will judge you, you wicked [or slothful] servant' (Luke 19:22). 'You said I was this or that. Why then did you not put my money in the bank?' (v. 23). 'Cast the unprofitable servant into the outer darkness. There will be weeping and gnashing of teeth' (Matt. 25:30).

1. What shall I say? Time is passing, and will you be slothful?

2. Much of your lives has already passed, and will you be slothful?

3. Your souls are worth a thousand worlds, and will you be slothful?

4. The day of death and judgement is at the door, and will you be slothful?

5. The curse of God hangs over your head, and will you be slothful?

6. Besides this, the demons are in earnest, labouring and seeking by every means, every day, by every sin, to keep you out of heaven and to deprive you of salvation; and will you be slothful?

7. Your neighbours diligently seek the things that will perish, and will you be slothful concerning the things that will endure for ever?

8. Would you be willing to be damned for slothfuness?

9. Would you be willing for the angels of God to neglect to carry your souls away to heaven when you lie dying, and rather for the demons to stand by ready to scramble for them?

10. Was Christ slothful in the work of your redemption?

11. Are his ministers slothful in making this known to you?

12. And lastly, if all this will not move you, I tell you, God will not be slothful or negligent to damn you, whose damnation has for a long time *not* been slumbering. The demons will not neglect to come and get you, nor will hell neglect to shut its mouth upon you.

Sluggard, are you still asleep? Are you resolved to sleep the sleep of death? Will neither tidings from heaven nor hell awaken you? Will you still say, 'A little sleep, a little slumber, a little folding of the hands to sleep'? (Prov. 6:10). Will you yet turn yourself in your sloth, as a door turns itself upon its hinges? Oh, that I was one that was skilful in lamentation, and had a yearning heart for you, how I would pity you! How I would weep for you! Oh, that I could with Jeremiah let my eyes run down with rivers of tears for you! Poor soul, lost soul, dying soul, what a hard heart have I that I cannot mourn for you! If you should lose only a limb, a child, or a friend, it would not be so much; but, poor man, it is your soul! If it were to lie in hell just for a day, just for a year, no, ten thousand years, it would, in comparison, be nothing. But, oh, it is for ever! Oh, this cutting word *ever*! What terrifying words for the soul will those be which say, 'Depart from me, you cursed, into the everlasting fire!' (Matt. 25:41).

*Objection*:

But if I were to get started, and run as you would have me, then I must run from all my friends, for none of them are running that way.

*Answer*:

And if you do, you will run into the bosom of Christ and of God, and what harm will that do you?

*Objection*:

But if I run this way, then I must run from all my sins.

*Answer*:

That is true indeed. Yet if you do not, you will run into hell-fire.

*Objection*:

But if I run this way, I shall be hated and lose the love of my friends and relations, and of those that I expect to bene-fit from, or am reliant upon, and I shall also be mocked by all my neighbours.

*Answer*:

If you do not, then you are sure to lose the love and favour of God and of Christ, the benefit of heaven and glory, and to be mocked by God for your folly: 'I also will laugh at your calamity; I will mock when your terror comes' (Prov. 1:26). And if you would not want to be hated and mocked, then take heed that by your folly you do not procure the displeasure and mockings of the great God; for his mockings and hatred will be terrible because they will fall upon you in terrible times, even when tribulation and anguish take hold of you, which will be when death and judgement comes, when all the men on earth and all the angels in heaven will not be able to help you (Prov. 1:26-28).

*Objection*:
But surely I may begin this at some future time, a year or two from now, may I not?

*Answer*:
First, do you know the length of your days? Did God ever tell you that you would live half a year, or even two months longer? No, it may be you might not live even that long. And therefore second, will you be so foolish and unwise as to risk your soul upon a little time which is uncertain? Third, do you know whether the day of grace will last another week longer or not? For the day of grace has passed with some before their life has ended; and if it should be so with you, would you not say, 'Oh, if only I had begun to run before the day of grace had passed and the gates of heaven were shut against me!'? But, fourth, if you saw any of your neighbours neglecting to make certain the possession of either house or land, if these were offered to them, saying, 'There's time enough for that later,' when the time is uncertain, and besides, when they do not know whether or not it will ever be offered to them again; would you not call them fools? And if so, do you then think that you are a wise man to let your immortal soul hang over hell by a thread of uncertain time, which may soon be cut asunder by death?

But to speak plainly, all these are the words of a slothful spirit. Arise, man, be slothful no longer. Set foot and heart and all into the way of God, and run; for the crown is at the end of the race, where also stands the loving Forerunner, even Jesus, who has prepared heavenly provision to make your soul welcome. And he will give it to you with a heart more willing than ever you could desire it from him. Oh, therefore do not delay any longer, but put into practice the words of the men of Dan to their brothers after they had seen the goodness of the land of Canaan, 'Arise... For we have seen the land, and indeed it is very good. Would you do nothing? Do not hesitate to go, and enter to possess the land' (Judg. 18:9).

Farewell.

I hope our souls meet in comfort at the journey's end.

John Bunyan

# I

## Heaven must be run for

*Run in such a way that you may obtain it (1 Cor. 9:24)*

Heaven and happiness is what everyone desires, so much so that even wicked Balaam could say, 'Let me die the death of the righteous, and let my end be like his!' (Num. 23:10). Yet for all this, there are very few who do obtain that ever-to-be-desired glory, inasmuch as many eminent among those who profess faith fall short of a welcome from God into this pleasant place.

Therefore, because he desired the salvation of the souls of the Corinthians, to whom he wrote this epistle, the apostle lays before them such counsel in these words, which if taken, would be for their help and advantage.

First, [they were] not to be wicked and sit still and wish for heaven, but to run for it. Second, [they were] not to content themselves with every kind of running, but, as he says, to 'run in such a way that [they] may obtain it.' As if he should say, 'Some, because they would not lose their souls, begin to run in good time' (Eccles. 12:1). They run swiftly; they run with patience; they run the right way (Heb. 12:1). Do you run in this way? Some run from both father and mother, friends and companions in order to obtain the crown. Do you run in such a way? Some run through temptations, afflictions, good report, evil report in order that they may win the pearl (1 Cor. 4:11-13; 2 Cor. 6:1-10). Do you run in this way? 'Run in such a way that you may obtain it.'

These words are taken from men's running for a prize — a very apt illustration to set before the eyes of the saints of the Lord. 'Do you not know that those who run in a race all run, but one receives the prize? Run in such a way that you may obtain it' (1 Cor. 9:24). That means do not just run, but be sure that you win as well as run: 'Run in such a way that you may obtain it.'

I shall not need to make any great ado in opening up these words at this time, but I shall rather set before you one doctrine that I find in them; and in doing so I shall show you, in some measure, the meaning and intent of these words.


## 1. The doctrine of the text

The doctrine is this: those who will gain heaven must run for it; I repeat, those who will gain heaven must run for it! I beg you to heed my words well. 'Do you not know that those who run in a race all run, but one receives the prize?' See to it that you run in this way. The prize is heaven; and if you wish to obtain it, you must run for it. You have another scripture for this in Hebrews 12:1: 'Therefore we also,' says the apostle, 'since we are surrounded by so great a cloud of witnesses, let us lay aside every weight, and the sin which so easily ensnares us, and let us run with endurance the race that is set before us.' 'And let us run,' says he. Again, says Paul, 'I run thus: not with uncertainty. Thus I fight, etc.' (1 Cor. 9:26).

## 2. The word *run* explained

But before I go any further, please note, first, *fleeing*. This
running is not an ordinary sort, or any sort, of running, but
it is to be understood to be of the swiftest sort of running;
and therefore in Hebrews chapter 6, it is called a *fleeing*:
'...we might have strong consolation, who have *fled* for
refuge to lay hold of the hope set before us' (v. 18). Take
note of who it is who has fled. It is taken from Joshua chapter 20, which concerns the man who was to flee to the 'city
of refuge', when the 'avenger of blood' was hard at his heels,
to take vengeance on him for the offence that he had committed. Therefore, it is a running or fleeing for one's life — a
running with all 'might and main', as we are accustomed to
saying. See to it that you run in this way.

Second,[please note,] *pressing*. In another text, this running is called a *pressing*: 'I press towards the goal' (Phil.
3:14), which signifies that those who desire to gain heaven
must not stop at any difficulties they may meet with, but
they must press, push and thrust through all that may stand
between heaven and their souls. See to it that you run in
this way.

Third, [please note,] *continuing*. This running is called
in another text a *continuing* in the way of life: 'If indeed
you continue in the faith, grounded and steadfast, and *are*
not moved away from the hope of the gospel' (Col. 1:23).
This is not to run a little now and then, by fits and starts, or
half way or almost there, but to run for your life, to run
through all difficulties, and to continue running to the end
of the race, which must be to the end of your life: 'Run in
such a way that you may obtain it.'

## 3. Several reasons for expounding this doctrine

And the reasons for this point are these: first, because all
or every one who runs does not obtain the prize. There are
many who run, yes, and run a long way too, but who still
miss the crown that waits at the end of the race. You know
that all who run in a race do not obtain the victory; they all
run, but only one wins. And so is it here. It is not every one
who runs, nor every one who seeks, nor every one that
strives for the mastery that gets it (Luke 13:24-27). 'If anyone competes in athletics,' says Paul, 'he is not crowned
unless he competes according to the rules' (2 Tim. 2:5) —
that is, unless he runs and strives in such a way as to gain
God's approval. What, do you think that every heavy-heeled
person who professes faith will obtain heaven? What, every
lazy one, every careless and foolish one, who is stopped by
anything, kept back by anything, who hardly runs as fast
heavenward as a snail creeps along the ground? No, there
are some who profess to be in the faith who do not go as
fast in the way of God as a snail does along a wall, and yet,
they think that heaven and happiness will be theirs. But
wait, there are many more who run than there are who
obtain; therefore, he who would obtain heaven must run
for it.

Second, because you know that though a man runs, yet,
if he does not overcome or win as well as run, how will he
be the better for his running? He will get nothing. You know
the man who runs does it so that he may win the prize. But
if he does not obtain it, he has lost his labours, spent his
time and energy, and to no purpose. I say, he gets nothing.
And, ah, how many such runners will be found on the Day

of Judgement! Even multitudes, multitudes who have run, yes, multitudes who have run so far as to reach the gates of heaven, and yet, are not able to get any further, but stand there knocking when it is too late, crying, 'Lord, Lord!', when they have nothing but rebukes for their efforts: 'Depart from me! You cannot come in here; you have come too late; you ran too lazily. The door is shut!' 'When once the Master of the house has risen up,' says Christ, 'and shut the door, and you begin to stand outside and knock at the door, saying, "Lord, Lord, open for us," and he will answer and say to you, "I do not know you... Depart from me, etc."' (Luke 13:25,27). Oh, sad will be the state of those who run and miss. Therefore, if you would obtain heaven, you must run for it; so, 'Run in such a way that you may obtain it.'

Third, because the way is long (I speak metaphorically) and there is many a muddy step, many a steep hill, much work to do, a wicked heart, world and devil to overcome. I say, there are many steps to be taken by those who intend to be saved, by running or walking in the steps of that faith of our father Abraham. Out of Egypt, you must go through the Red Sea. You must run a long and tedious journey through the vast howling wilderness before you come to the promised land.

Fourth, those who would get to heaven must run for it because, just as the way is long, so the time in which they have to get to the end is very uncertain. The present time is the only time. You have no more time allotted to you than what you now enjoy: 'Do not boast about tomorrow, for you do not know what a day may bring forth' (Prov. 27:1). Do not say, 'I have time enough to get to heaven seven years from now,' for I tell you, the bell may toll for you before seven more days have passed. And when death comes, away you must go, whether you are ready for it or not; and therefore, pay attention to it; do not delay; it is not good dallying with things of such great concern as the salvation or damnation of your soul. You know that he who has a long way to go in a short time, and less than half the time that he thinks he has, had better run for it!

Fifth, those who would get to heaven must run for it, because the devil, the law, sin, death and hell follow them. There is never a poor soul who is going to heaven that the devil, the law, sin, death and hell do not go in pursuit of: 'Your adversary the devil walks about like a roaring lion, seeking whom he may devour' (1 Peter 5:8). And I can assure you that the devil is nimble; he can run swiftly; he is fleet of foot, and has overtaken many, has tripped them and has given them an everlasting fall. Also, the law can shoot a long way. Take care that you keep out of the reach of those great guns: the Ten Commandments. Hell also has a wide mouth; it can stretch itself further than you are aware of, as the angel said to Lot, 'Do not look behind you nor stay anywhere in the plain [that is, anywhere between here and heaven] ... lest you be destroyed' (Gen. 19:17). So I say to you, take heed; do not delay, lest either the devil, hell, death, or the fearful curses of the law of God overtake you and throw you down in the midst of your sins, so that you never rise and recover again. If this were well considered, then you, as well as I, would say, 'Those who will gain heaven must run for it.'

Sixth, those who desire to go to heaven must run for it because the gates of heaven may be shut shortly. Sometimes sinners do not have heaven's gates open to them for as long as they suppose; and if they are ever shut against a man, they are so heavy that all the men in the world and all the angels in heaven are not able to open them. 'I shut, and no man can open,' says Christ. And what if you should come only a quarter of an hour too late? I tell you it will cost you an eternity in which to bemoan your misery. Francis Spira can tell you what it is to wait till the gate of mercy is quite shut, or to run so lazily that they are shut before you get inside them. What, to be shut out! What, out of heaven! Sinner, rather than lose it, run for it, yes, and 'Run in such a way that you may obtain it.'

Seventh, and lastly, because if you lose, you lose all. You lose your soul, God, Christ, heaven, ease, peace, etc. Besides, you lay yourself open to all the shame, contempt and reproach that either God, Christ, the saints, the world, sin, the devil, and all can lay upon you. As Christ says of the foolish builder, so will I say of you, if you are such a one who runs and misses, I say, even all those who pass by will begin to mock you, saying, 'This man began [to run well but] was not able to finish.' (See Luke 14:28-30.) But more of this anon.


*Question*:

But how should a poor soul run? For this is the very thing that sorely afflicts me, as you say, to think that I may run and still fall short. To fall short at the last, I think, is what causes me great fear. I beg you, tell me, therefore, how I should run.

*Answer*:

That you may indeed be satisfied on this point, consider these nine directions on how to run.

# *II*

## Nine directions on how to run

### *The first direction*

If you wish to run so as to obtain the kingdom of heaven, then be sure that you get into the way that leads there; for it is a vain thing to think that you will ever get the prize, unless you are in the way that leads to it, even though you run ever so fast. Consider the case of a man in London who, for a prize, was to run to York. Now, though he runs ever so swiftly, yet, if he runs in a southerly direction, he could run himself quickly out of breath and still be no nearer the prize, but rather the further off. It is just so here; it is not simply the runner, nor even the speedy runner that wins the crown, unless he is in the way that leads to it. I have observed in the little time that I have professed faith that there is a lot of running to and fro, some this way and some that way; yet, it is to be feared that most of them are out of the way, and then, though they run as swiftly as an eagle can fly, they gain no benefit at all.

Here is one who runs 'a-Quaking' [a reference to the early Quakers] and another 'a-ranting'. [The ranters were an extreme sect of those days.] Again, one runs after baptism and another after Independency. Here is one for 'free will' and another for presbytery, and yet, quite possibly most of all these sects are running in quite the wrong way. Yet, every one is for his life, his soul, either for heaven or hell.

If you now say, 'Which is the way?' I tell you it is Christ, the Son of Mary, the Son of God. Jesus says, 'I am the way, the truth, and the life. No one comes to the Father except through me' (John 14:6). So, then your business is, if you would have salvation, to see if Christ is yours with all his benefits, whether he has covered you with his righteousness, whether he has shown you that your sins are washed away by his blood, whether you are rooted in him, and whether you have faith in him, so as to receive your life from him and to be conformed to him. That is the faith that enables you to conclude that you are righteous because Christ is your righteousness, and so to be constrained to walk with him as the joy of your heart because he has saved your soul. And for the Lord's sake, take heed and do not deceive yourself, and think that you are in the way upon grounds that are too slender. For if you miss the way, you will miss the prize, and if you miss that, I am sure you will lose your soul, even that soul which is worth more than the whole world. But I have dealt with this in more detail in my book on the two covenants, and shall therefore pass over it for now. I only beg you to be concerned for your soul, and in order that you may do so, take this counsel: do not trust in your own strength; throw it away. Go down on your knees in prayer to the Lord for the Spirit of truth. Search his Word for direction. Flee the company of seducers; keep company with mature Christians who have the most experience of Christ. And be sure to be on your guard against Quakers, ranters, free-willers. Also, do not keep too much company with some Anabaptists, although I go under that name myself! I tell you, this is such a serious matter, and I fear you will have so little regard for it that thoughts of the value of the thing and of your regarding it too lightly even make my heart ache while I am writing to you. May the Lord teach you the way by his Spirit, and then I am sure you will know it. See to it that you run in this way.

Let me urge you, in passing, to beware of two things and then I shall move on to the next direction:

1. Beware of relying on outward obedience to any of God's commands, or of thinking yourself to be better in the sight of God for it.

2. Beware of obtaining peace for your soul from any inherent righteousness. But if you can believe that as you are a sinner, so are you justified freely by the love of God, through the redemption that is in Christ; and that God for Christ's sake has forgiven you, not because he saw anything done, or that would be done in you or by you, to move him to do it; for that is the right way; it was the Lord who put you into the way and will keep you in it!

*The second direction*

As you should get into the way, so you should also be much in study and reflecting on the way. You know that men who wish to be expert in anything are usually much in the study of that thing; so it is with those that quickly become expert in anything. This, therefore, is what you should do. Let your study be much concerned with Christ, who is the way: what he is; what he has done; why he is what he is; and why he has done what is done, such as why he took upon himself 'the form of a bondservant', why he was made 'in the likeness of men' (Phil 2:7), why he cried, why he died, why he bore the sins of the world, why he was made sin, why he was made righteousness, why he is in heaven bearing the nature of man, and what he is doing there (2 Cor. 5:21). Be much in reflection upon and consideration of these things. Also be thinking often of those places which you must not come near, but leave some on this hand and some on that. As it is with those who travel in other countries, who have to avoid a particular gate on this hand, and such a bush on that hand, and pass by such a place where such a thing is standing. This therefore is what you must do: avoid such things which are expressly forbidden in the Word of God. 'Remove your way far from her, and do not go near the door of her house' (Prov. 5:8). 'Her house is the way to hell, descending to the chambers of death' (Prov. 7:27). And so it is with everything that is not in the way; beware of it so that you do not go by it. Do not come near it; have nothing to do with it. See to it that you run in this way.

### The third direction

Not only this, but in the next place, you must strip yourself of those things that may cling to you and hinder your progress in the way to the kingdom of heaven, things, such as covetousness, pride, lust, or whatever else your heart may be inclined towards and which may hinder you in this heavenly race. Men that run for a prize, if they intend to win as well as run, do not usually burden themselves, or carry those things on them that may be a hindrance to them in their running. 'And everyone who competes for the prize is temperate in all things' (1 Cor. 9:25) — that is, he lays aside every thing that would be in any way a disadvantage to him, as the apostle says, 'Let us lay aside every weight, and the sin which so easily ensnares us, and let us run with endurance the race that is set before us' (Heb. 12:1). It is but a vain thing to talk of going to heaven if you let your heart be burdened with those things that would hinder you. Would you not say that, though he runs, such a man is in danger of losing if he fills his pockets with stones, wears heavy garments on his shoulders and big heavy shoes on his feet? It is the same here; you talk of going to heaven and yet fill your pockets with stones — that is, you fill your heart with this world and let it hang on your shoulders with its profits and pleasures. Alas, alas, you are greatly mistaken! If you intend to win, you must strip, you must lay aside every weight, you must be temperate in all things. That is how you must run.

### The fourth direction

Beware of side-paths. Take care that you do not turn into those lanes which lead out of the way. There are crooked paths, paths in which men go astray, paths that lead to death and damnation; beware of all those (Isa. 59:8; Prov. 7:25). Some of them are dangerous because of practice, others because of popular opinion, but do not give them any consideration. Consider the path before you; look straight ahead; turn neither to the right nor to the left; but let your eyes look straight ahead (Prov. 3:17). 'Ponder the path of your feet, and let all your ways be established. Do not turn to the right or the left; remove your foot from evil' (Prov. 4:26-27). This counsel not taken as seriously as it is given is the reason for that shifting from opinion to opinion, reeling this way and that way, out of this lane into that lane, and so missing the way to the kingdom. Though the way to heaven is but one way, yet, there are many crooked lanes and side-paths which bear down upon it, as I might say. And again, notwithstanding the fact that the kingdom of heaven is the biggest city, yet, usually those side-paths are the most trodden. Most travellers go those ways, and therefore the way to heaven is hard to find, and as hard to be kept in because of these side-paths. Yet, nevertheless, it is in this case as it was with the harlot of Jericho; she had one scarlet thread tied in her window by which her house was

known (Josh. 2:18). So it is here, the scarlet streams of
Christ's blood run throughout the way to the kingdom of
heaven; therefore, look for that. See if you can find the
sprinkling of the blood of Christ in the way, and if you do,
be of good cheer, you are in the right way. But take care
that you do not deceive yourself with a fanciful notion, for
then you may turn into any lane or way. But in order that
you may not be mistaken, consider this: that though it seems
ever so pleasant, if you do not find that in the very middle
of the road there is writing with the heart-blood of Christ
that states that 'Christ Jesus came into the world to save
sinners' and that we are justified though we are ungodly,
then shun that way. For this is what the apostle means when
he says, 'Therefore, brethren, having boldness to enter the
holiest by the blood of Jesus, by a new and living way which
he consecrated for us, through the veil, that is, his flesh'
(Heb. 10:19-20).

How easy a matter it is in this day for the devil to be too
cunning for poor souls by calling his side-paths the way to
the kingdom! If such an opinion or fanciful idea is but cried
out by one or more, and this inscription set upon it by the
devil, 'This is the way of God,' how speedily, greedily, and
by heaps do poor, simple souls throw themselves away upon
it, especially if it is daubed over with a few external acts of
morality — if so good! But this is because men do not dis-
cern dressed-up, decorated side-paths from the plain way
to the kingdom of heaven. They have not yet learned the
true Christ, and what his righteousness is. Neither have
they a sense of their own insufficiency, but are bold, proud,
presumptuous, and self-conceited. And therefore,

### The fifth direction

Do not look upwards too much in your journey heaven-
wards. You know that men who run in a race do not usually

stare and gaze this way and that. Neither do they usually lift up their eyes too high, lest perhaps, by their gazing too much at other things, they in the meantime stumble and catch a fall. The very same situation is this: if you gaze and stare after every opinion and way that comes into the world, also if you pry overmuch into God's secret decrees, or let your heart entertain questions about some nice, foolish curiosities too much, you may stumble and fall, as many hundreds in England have done, both in following the ranters and the Quakers, to their own eternal overthrow, without the marvellous operation of God's grace suddenly stretched forth to bring them back again.

Take heed therefore and follow not that proud, lofty spirit that, devil-like, cannot be content with its own station. David was of an excellent spirit when he said, 'LORD my heart is not haughty, nor my eyes lofty. Neither do I concern myself with great matters, nor with things too profound for me. Surely I have calmed and quieted my soul, like a weaned child with his mother; like a weaned child is my soul within me' (Ps. 131:1-2). See to it that you run in this way.

### The sixth direction

Take heed that you do not have an ear open to everyone that calls after you as you are on your journey. Men who run, you know, if anyone calls after them, saying, 'I would speak with you,' or, 'Do not go too fast and you shall have my company,' if they are running for some great reason, they usually say, 'Sorry, I cannot stop; I am in a hurry; I beg you not to talk to me now; neither can I wait for you because I am running for a prize. If I win, I am made; if I lose, I am undone; and therefore do not hinder me.' So wise are men when they run for corruptible things, and so should you do; and you have more cause to do so than they;

inasmuch as they run only for things that do not last, but
you for an incorruptible glory. I give you timely notice of
this knowing that you will have plenty calling after you,
even the devil, sin, this world, vain company, pleasure,
profits, esteem among men, ease, pomp, pride, together with
an innumerable company of such companions. One crying,
'Wait for me!' Another saying, 'Do not leave me behind!' A
third saying, 'Take me along with you!' 'What, will you go,'
says the devil, 'without your sins, pleasures and profits?
Are you in such a rush? Can you not wait and take these
along with you? Will you leave your friends and companions
behind you? Can you not do as your neighbours do: carry
the world, sin, lust, pleasure, profit, esteem among men
along with you?' Take care that you do not let your ear now
be open to the tempting, enticing, alluring and soul-
entangling flatteries of such soul-sinkers as these are. 'My
son,' says Solomon, 'if sinners entice you, do not consent'
(Prov. 1:10). You know what it cost the young man whom
Solomon speaks of in the seventh chapter of Proverbs, who
was enticed by a harlot: 'With her enticing speech she
caused him to yield, with her flattering lips she seduced
him. Immediately he went after her, as an ox goes to the
slaughter, or as a fool to the correction of the stocks, till an
arrow struck his liver. As a bird hastens to the snare, he did
not know it would cost his life. Now therefore, listen to me
my children; pay attention to the words of my mouth: do
not let your heart turn aside to her ways, do not stray into
her paths; for she has cast down many wounded, and all
who were slain by her were strong men. Her house is the
way to hell, descending to the chambers of death' (Prov.
7:21-27). Soul, take this counsel and say, 'Satan, sin, lust,
pleasure, profit, pride, friends, companions, and everything
else, leave me alone; stand back; do not come near me, for
I am running for heaven, for my soul, for God, for Christ,

from hell and everlasting damnation. If I win, I win all; and if I lose, I lose all; therefore, leave me alone for I will not listen. See to it that you run in this way.

## The seventh direction

In the next place, do not be daunted even though you meet with ever so many discouragements in your journey there. The man who is resolved to get to heaven, if Satan cannot win him by flatteries, he will endeavour to weaken him by discouragements, saying, 'You are a sinner; you have broken God's law. You are not one of the elect; you have come too late; the day of grace has passed. God does not care about you; your heart is nothing; you are lazy' — and with a hundred other discouraging suggestions. And so it was with David when he said, 'I would have lost heart, unless I had believed that I would see the goodness of the Lord in the land of the living' (Ps. 27:13). It is as if he should say, 'The devil did so rage, and my heart was so base, that had I judged according to my own senses and feelings I would have been absolutely distracted. But I entrusted myself to Christ in the promise and looked to God, considering that he would be as good as his promise, in having mercy upon me an unworthy sinner. And this is what encouraged me and kept me from fainting.' And this is what you must do when Satan, and the law, and your own conscience try to dishearten you, either by the greatness of your sins, the wickedness of your heart, the tediousness of the way, the loss of outward enjoyments, the hatred that you will receive from the world, or the like. Then you must encourage yourself with the freeness of the promises, the tender-heartedness of Christ, the merits of his blood, the freeness of his invitations to you to come in, the greatness of the sin of others who have been pardoned; and also that the same God through the same Christ holds forth the same grace as free as ever. If these are not your meditations, you will progress very slowly in the way to heaven, if you do not give up all as lost, and so knock off from following any further. Therefore, I say, take heart in your journey and say to those who seek your destruction, 'Do not rejoice over me, my enemy; when I fall, I will arise; when I sit in darkness, the LORD will be a light to me' (Micah 7:8). See to it that you run in this way.

### The eighth direction

Take heed not to be offended at the cross that you must go by before you reach heaven. You must understand, as I have already touched upon, that there is no man who goes to heaven who does not have to go by the cross. The cross is the mark on the way by which all those who go to glory must pass by: 'We must through many tribulations enter the kingdom of God (Acts 14:22). 'Yes, and all who desire to live godly in Christ Jesus will suffer persecution' (2 Tim. 3:12). If you are in the way to the kingdom, my life for yours, you will come to the cross shortly. May the Lord grant it that you do not shrink from it so that you turn back again! 'If anyone desires to come after me,' says Christ, 'let him deny himself, and take up his cross daily, and follow me' (Luke 9:23). The cross stands and has stood from the beginning as a mark on the way to the kingdom of heaven. You know if one asks you the way to such and such a place, in order to give better directions, you do not only say, 'This is the way,' but you also say, 'You must go by such a gate, and such a stile, such a bush, tree, bridge and the like.' Why, it is the same here. Are you inquiring concerning the way to heaven? Why, I tell you, Christ is the way. Into him you must get, into his righteousness in order to be justified. And if you are in him, you will presently see the cross.

You must go close by it; you must touch it. Not only that, you must take it up or else you will quickly go out of the way that leads to heaven and turn up some of those crooked lanes that lead down to the chambers of death. Now you may know the cross by these six things: (1) it is known in the doctrine of justification, (2) in the doctrine of mortification, (3) in the doctrine of perseverance, (4) in self-denial, (5) patience, (6) communion with poor saints.

1. In the doctrine of justification, there is a great deal of the cross. A man is forced to suffer the destruction of his own righteousness for the righteousness of another. This is no easy matter for a man to do. I assure you, it stretches every vein in his heart before he will be brought to yield to it. What, for a man to deny, reject, abhor, and throw away all his prayers, tears, alms, keeping of sabbaths, hearing, reading, and the rest, in the matter of justification! To count them accursed and to be willing in the very midst of the consciousness of his sins, to throw himself wholly upon the righteousness and obedience of another man, abhorring his own righteousness, counting it as deadly sin, as the open breach of the law! I say, to do this in deed and in truth is the biggest piece of the cross. And therefore Paul calls this very thing a 'suffering' when he says, 'I have suffered the loss of all things [which was chiefly his righteousness] ... that I may gain Christ and be found in him, not having [but rejecting] my own righteousness' (Phil. 3:8-9). That is the first thing.

2. In the doctrine of mortification, there is also much of the cross. Is it nothing for a man to lay hands on his vile opinions, on his vile sins, on his bosom sins, on his beloved, pleasant, darling sins, that stick as close to him as the flesh sticks to the bones? What, to lose all these brave things that my eyes behold for that which I never saw with my eyes! What, to lose all these splendid things that my

eyes behold for that which I never saw with my eyes! What, to lose my pride, my covetousness, my vain company, sports and pleasures, and all the rest! I tell you this is no easy matter. If it were, then what need would there be of all those prayers, sighs, watchings? What would be the need to shrink back from it? No, do you not see that before some men will set about this work, they will even risk the loss of their souls, heaven, God, Christ, and all? What else do all those delays and put-offs mean, saying, 'Wait a little longer; I am reluctant to leave my sins while I am so young and healthy'? Again, what other reason is there why others do it only by halves, coldly and seldom, notwithstanding that they are convinced over and over again; and not only that, they also promise to amend, and yet all is in vain? I can assure you that to cut off right hands and to pluck out right eyes is no pleasure to the flesh.

3. The doctrine of perseverance is also a cross to the flesh. This is not only to begin but also to hold on; not only to bid well and to say, 'I would like to have heaven,' but to know Christ, to put on Christ, and to walk with Christ so as to reach heaven. Indeed, it is no great matter to begin to look for heaven, to begin to seek the Lord, to begin to shun sin. Oh, but it is a very great matter to continue with God's approbation: 'My servant Caleb,' says God, 'because he has a different spirit in him and has followed me fully, I will bring into the land where he went, and his descendants shall inherit it' (Num. 14:24). Almost all the many thousands of the children of Israel in their generation fell short of perseverance when they walked from Egypt towards the land of Canaan. Indeed, they went to work at first pretty willingly, but they were very short-winded. They were quickly out of breath, and in their hearts they turned back again into Egypt. It is an easy matter for a man to run hard for a spurt, for a short distance, for a mile or two, but, oh, to

hold out for a hundred, for a thousand, for ten thousand miles. The man who does this must expect to meet with crosses, pain and weariness to the flesh, especially if, as he goes, he meets with briars and quagmires, and other encumbrances that make his journey so much the more painful.

No, do you not see daily with your eyes that perseverance is a very great part of the cross? Why else do men soon grow so weary? I could point out many who after they have followed the ways of God for about twelve months, and others maybe only two, three or four years, some more, some less, have been beaten out of wind, have taken up their lodging and rest before they have got halfway to heaven. Some have become entangled in this sin and some in that; and some have secretly, no, sometimes openly, said that the way is too narrow, the race too long, the religion too holy, and they cannot hold out; they can go no further. And the same with the other three, namely, patience, self-denial, communion and fellowship with and to the poor saints. How hard are these things? It is an easy matter to deny another man, but it is not so easy a matter to deny oneself. To deny myself of this advantage and of that gain out of love to God, to his gospel, to his saints, no, of that which, otherwise, I might lawfully do were it not for offending them! That scripture is but seldom read, and even more seldom put into practice which says, 'Therefore, if food makes my brother stumble, I will never again eat meat' (1 Cor. 8:13). Again, 'We then who are strong ought to bear with the scruples of the weak, and not to please ourselves' (Rom. 15:1). But how perverse, how hasty, how peevish and selfishly resolved, generally speaking, are those who profess to be believers these days. Alas, how little consideration for the poor, unless it is to say, 'Be warmed and filled.' But to give is rare, especially in giving to any that are poor

(Gal. 6:10). I tell you, all things are a cross to flesh and blood, and the man who has a watchful eye over the flesh and also some considerable measure of strength against it, shall find his heart in these things to be like a horse that has not been broken in, that is ridden without a curbing bridle, ready to start at everything that is offensive to him. Yes, and ready to run away too, no matter what the rider does! It is the cross which prevents those who do not get to heaven. I am persuaded that were it not for the cross, where we have only one who professes faith, we would have twenty. But this cross is what spoils it all!

Some men, as I said before, when they come to the cross, they can go no further, but back again to their sins they must go. Others stumble at it and break their necks. Others again, when they see that the cross is approaching, they turn aside to the left hand or the right hand, and so think to get to heaven another way; but they will be deceived. 'Yes, and all who desire to live godly in Christ Jesus will [note, *will*] suffer persecution' (2 Tim. 3:12). There are but few who cry, when they come to the cross, 'Welcome cross,' as some of the martyrs did to the stake they were burned at. Therefore, if you meet with the cross in your journey, in whatever manner it may be, do not be daunted and say, 'Alas, what shall I do now?' Rather take courage, knowing that the way to the kingdom is by the cross. Can a man believe in Christ and not be hated by the devil? Can he make a pleasing and convincing profession of Christ and the children of the devil hold their tongue? Can darkness agree with light? Can the devil tolerate that Christ Jesus should be honoured both by faith and by heavenly conduct, and leave that soul alone in peace? Did you ever read that '[the dragon] persecuted the woman' (Rev. 12:13) and that Christ said, 'In the world you will have tribulation'? (John 16:33).

## The ninth direction

Plead with God that he would do these two things for you: first, enlighten your understanding, and second, inflame your will. If these two are but effectually done, then there is no fear; you will go safely to heaven.

First, enlighten your understanding. One of the great reasons why men and women have so little regard for the other world is because they see so little of it. And the reason why they see so little of it is because they have their understanding darkened. And therefore Paul says to the believers, 'You should no longer walk as the rest of the Gentiles walk, in the futility of their mind, having their understanding darkened, being alienated from the life of God, because of the ignorance [or foolishness] that is in them, because of the blindness of their heart' (Eph. 4:17-18). Walk not as they do; do not run with them. Poor souls, they also have their understandings darkened, their hearts blinded, and that is the reason why they have such undervaluing thoughts of the Lord Jesus Christ and the salvation of their souls. For when men come to see the things of another world — what a God, what a Christ, what a heaven and what an eternal glory there is to be enjoyed; also when they see that it is possible for them to have a share in it, I tell you, it will make them run through thick and thin to enjoy it. Moses having a sight of this, because his understanding was enlightened, did not fear 'the wrath of the king' (Heb. 11:27), but chose 'rather to suffer affliction with the people of God than to enjoy the passing pleasures of sin' (Heb. 11:25). He refused to be called the son of the king's daughter, esteeming it wonderful riches to be accounted worthy of so much as to suffer for Christ with the poor, despised saints. And that was because he saw him who was invisible and 'looked to the reward' (Heb. 11:26-27). And this is what the apostle

usually prayed for the saints in his epistles, namely, 'That
[they] may know what is the hope of his calling, what are
the riches of the glory of his inheritance in the saints' (Eph.
1:18), and that they 'may be able to comprehend with all
the saints what is the width and length and depth and height
— to know the love of Christ which passes knowledge' (Eph.
3:18-19). Pray therefore that God would enlighten your
understanding; that will be a very great help to you. It will
help you to endure many a hard blow for Christ. As Paul
says, 'After you were illuminated, you endured a great
struggle with sufferings ... and joyfully accepted the
plundering of your goods, knowing that you have a better
and an enduring possession for yourselves in heaven' (Heb.
10:32-34). If there were ever such a rare jewel just in a man's
path, if he does not see it, will he not rather trample upon
it than stoop down for it? And this is because he does not
see it. Why, so it is here. Though heaven be worth ever so
much and you have ever so much need of it, yet if you do
not see it — that is, have not your understanding opened or
enlightened to see — then you will not have any regard for
it at all. Therefore, cry to the Lord for enlightening grace,
and say, 'Lord, open my blind eyes. Lord, take the veil off
my dark heart. Show me the things of the other world, and
let me see the beauty, glory and excellency of them for
Christ's sake.' This is the first thing.

Second, inflame your will. Cry to God also that he would
inflame your will with the things of the other world. For
when a man's will is fully set to do one thing or another,
then it must be a very big matter that shall hinder that man
from achieving his goal. When Paul's will was firmly resolved to go up to Jerusalem, though it was signified to him
beforehand what he would suffer there, yet he was not
daunted at all, no, he said, 'I am ready not only to be bound,
but also to die at Jerusalem for the name of the Lord Jesus'

(Acts 21:13). His will was inflamed with love to Christ, and therefore all the persuasions that could be used achieved nothing at all.

Nobody knows what to do with your self-willed people. We used to say, 'He will have his own will, whatever you do.' Indeed, to have such a will for heaven is an admirable advantage to a man who embarks upon the race there. A man who is resolved and has his will fixed, says, 'I will do my best to give myself an advantage. I will do my worst to hinder my enemies. I will not give up as long as I can stand. I will have it or I will lose my life.' 'Though he slay me, yet will I trust him' (Job 13:15). 'I will not let you go unless you bless me!' (Gen. 32:26). *I will, I will, I will.* Oh, this blessed will inflamed for heaven! What is there like it? If a man is willing, then any argument shall be cause for encouragement; but if unwilling, then any argument shall be a cause of discouragement. This is seen both in saints and sinners, in those who are the children of God, and also in those who are the children of the devil. As, (1) the saints of old being willing and resolved for heaven, what could stop them? Could fire or stake, sword or halter, stinking dungeons, whips, bears, bulls, lions, cruel tortures, stoning, starving, nakedness, etc. stop them? (Heb. 11). And, 'in all these things [they were] more than conquerors, through him who loved [them]'(Rom. 8:37), who had also made them 'willing in the day of his power'. (2) See again, on the other side, the children of the devil, how many means of escape and loopholes they will have, because they are not willing. 'I have married a wife; I have a farm; I shall offend my landlord; I shall offend my master; I shall lose my trade; I shall lose my pride, my pleasures; I shall be mocked and scoffed at; therefore, I dare not come.' 'I,' says another, 'will wait till I am older, till my children have gone, till I have progressed a little in the world, till I have done this, that and the other business.' But, alas, the thing is that they are not willing, for were they but thoroughly willing, these and a thousand such as these would hold them more strongly than cords held Samson when he broke them like burnt flax (Judg. 15:14). I tell you, the will is all. That is one of the chief things which turns the wheel either backwards or forwards, and God knows that full well, and so likewise does the devil. Therefore, they both endeavour very much to strengthen the will of their servants. God is for making of his servants a willing people to serve him. The devil does what he can to possess the will and the affection of those who are his, with love to sin. And therefore when Christ comes close to the matter, he says, indeed, 'You are not willing to come to me' (John 5:40). 'How often I wanted to gather your children together, as a hen gathers her brood under her wings, but you were not willing!' (Luke 13:34). The devil had possessed their wills, and so long he was sure enough of them. Oh therefore cry hard to God to in-flame your will for heaven and Christ — your will, I say, if that is rightly set for heaven, you will not be beaten off with discouragements. Though he lost a limb, as it were, and the hollow of his thigh was put out of joint when he wrestled with the angel, this was the reason that, as he wrestled with him, Jacob said, 'I will not [note, *I will not*] let you go unless you bless me!' (Gen. 32:26). Get your will touched with the heavenly grace and the resolution against all discouragements, and then you will go full speed to-wards heaven. But if you falter in your will and are not sound there, you will run hobbling and halting all the way you run, and you are sure to fall short at the last. The Lord give you the will and courage!

Thus have I done with directing you how to run to the kingdom. Be sure that you keep in memory what I have said to you, lest you lose your way. But because I would have you think of them, consider them all in summary on this little bit of paper:

1. Get into the way.
2. Then study it.
3. Then strip and lay aside everything that would hinder.
4. Beware of side-paths.
5. Do not gaze and stare too much about you, but be sure to ponder the path of your feet.
6. Do not stop for any that call after you, whether it is the world, the flesh or the devil; for all these will hinder your journey, if possible.
7. Be not daunted with any discouragements you meet with as you go.
8. Take heed of stumbling at the cross.
9. Cry hard to God for an enlightened heart and a willing mind; and God give you a prosperous journey!

Yet, before I do quite take my leave of you, let me give you a few motives to take along with you. It may be that they will be as good a pair of spurs to encourage your sluggish heart in this rich journey.

# *III*

## Nine motives to urge us on in the way

### *The first motive*

Consider, there is no way but this — you must either win or lose. If you win, then heaven, God, Christ, glory, ease, peace, life, yes, life eternal will be yours. You shall be made equal to the angels in heaven. You shall sorrow no more, sigh no more, feel no more pain. You shall be out of the reach of sin, hell, death, the devil, the grave and whatever else may endeavour to hurt you. But, on the contrary, if you lose, then your loss is heaven, glory, God, Christ, ease, peace, and whatever else will accompany those things to make eternity comfortable to the saints. Besides, you procure eternal death, sorrow, pain, blackness, darkness, fellowship with demons, together with the everlasting damnation of your own soul.

### *The second motive*

Consider that this devil, this hell, death and damnation follow after you as hard as they can drive, and have their commission to do so by the law, against which you have sinned; and therefore, for the Lord's sake, make haste!

### The third motive

If they seize you before you get to the city of refuge, they will put an everlasting stop to your journey. This also cries, 'Run for it!'

### The fourth motive

Know, also, that now heaven's gates, the heart of Christ, with his arms, are wide open to receive you. Oh, I think this consideration, that the devil follows after to destroy, and that Christ stands open-armed to receive, should make you reach out and fly with all haste and speed. And therefore,

### The fifth motive

Keep your eye upon the prize. Be sure that your eyes are continually upon the profit you are likely to get. The reason why men are so apt to faint in their race for heaven lies chiefly in one of these two things: (1) they do not seriously consider the worth of the prize, or else if they do, they are afraid it is too good for them; but most lose heaven for the lack of considering the prize and the worth of it. And therefore that you may not do the same, keep your eye much upon the excellence, the pleasantness, the beauty, the comfort, the peace that is to be had there by those who win the prize. It was this that made the apostle run through anything: good report, evil report, persecution, affliction, hunger, nakedness, peril by sea and peril by land, bonds and imprisonments. Also, it made others endure being stoned, sawn asunder, to have their eyes bored with augurs, their bodies broiled on gridirons, their tongues cut out of their mouths, boiled in cauldrons, thrown to the wild beasts, burned at the stake, whipped at posts, and a thousand other fearful torments. 'While we do not look at the things which are seen [as the things of this world], but at the things which are not seen. For the things which are seen are temporary, but the things which are not seen are eternal' (2 Cor. 4:18). Oh, this word *eternal*! That was it that made them not accept deliverance, when they might have had it, for they knew that in the world to come they should have a better resurrection (Heb. 11:35). (2) And do not let thoughts of the rareness of the place make you say in your heart, 'This is too good for me.' For I tell you, heaven is prepared for whosoever will accept it, and they shall be received with a hearty good welcome. Consider this therefore that as badly as you have got there, there went worthless, beggarly Lazarus. No, it is prepared for the poor. 'Listen, my beloved brethren,' says James — take note of it — 'has God not chosen the poor of this world to be rich in faith and heirs of the kingdom?' (James 2:5). Therefore, take heart and run, man!

### The sixth motive

Think much of those who have gone on before. First, how they really got into the kingdom. Second, how safe they are in the arms of Jesus; would they be here again for a thousand worlds? Or, if they were, would they be afraid that God would not make them welcome? Third, what would they think of you if they knew that your heart began to fail you in your journey, or your sins began to allure you and to persuade you to stop your race? Would they not call you a thousand fools, and say, 'Oh, if only he saw what we see, felt what we feel, and tasted the dainties that we taste? Oh, if he were here one quarter of an hour to behold, to see, to feel, to taste and enjoy but the thousandth part of what we enjoy, what would he do? What would he suffer? What would he leave undone? Would he favour sin? Would he love this world below? Would he be afraid of friends, or shrink at the most fearful threatenings that the greatest tyrants could invent for him?' No, those who have had but a sight of these things by faith, when they have been as far away from them as heaven from earth, have been able to say with a comfortable and cheerful heart, as the bird that sings in the spring, that this and more shall not stop them from running to heaven. Sometimes, when my base heart has been inclined to this world and to loiter in my journey towards heaven, the very consideration of the glorious saints and angels in heaven — what they enjoy and what low thoughts they together have of the things of this world — how they would see me as a fool if they did but know that my heart was drawing back. This has caused me to rush onwards, to disdain these poor, low, empty, beggarly things, and to say to my soul, 'Come, soul, let us not be weary. Let us see what this heaven is. Let us even risk all for it, and see if that will redeem the cost.' Surely Abraham, David, Paul and the rest of the saints of God were as wise as any are now, and yet they lost all for this glorious kingdom. Oh, therefore throw away vile lusts; follow after righteousness; love the Lord Jesus; devote yourself to him in reverent fear. I shall guarantee you that he will give you a good reward. Reader, what do you say to this? Are you resolved to follow me? No, resolve, if you can, to get ahead of me. Run in such a way as to obtain.

*The seventh motive*

To encourage you a little further, begin the work and when you have run yourself weary, then the Lord Jesus will pick

you up and carry you. Is this not enough to make any poor
soul begin his race? Perhaps you cry, 'Oh, but I am feeble, I
am lame, etc.' Well, but Christ has a bosom. Consider this
therefore when you have run yourself weary, he will put
you in his bosom: 'He will gather the lambs with his arm,
and carry them in his bosom, and gently lead those who
are with young' (Isa. 40:11). This is what fathers use to encourage their children, saying, 'Run, sweet babe, until you
are weary, and then I will pick you up and carry you.' 'He
will gather the lambs with his arm, and carry them in his
bosom.' When they are weary, they shall ride.

### The eighth motive

Or else, he will convey new strength from heaven into your
soul, which will be as good; for, 'Even the youths shall faint
and be weary, and the young men shall utterly fall, but
those who wait on the LORD shall renew their strength; they
shall mount up with wings like eagles, they shall run and
not be weary, they shall walk and not faint' (Isa. 40:30-31).
What shall I say besides what has already been said? You
will have good and easy lodgings, a good and wholesome
diet, the bosom of Christ to lie on and the joys of heaven to
feed on. Shall I speak of the fulness and the duration of all
these? Truly, to describe them to their height is a work too
hard for me to do.

### The ninth motive

Again, I think the very industry of the devil and the industry of his servants should make you, who have a desire to
get to heaven and happiness, run swiftly. Why, the devil
will lose no time, spare no pains, neither will his servants
in seeking both the destruction of themselves and others.

And shall we not be as industrious for our own salvation? Shall the world risk the damnation of their souls for a poor, corruptible crown, and shall we not risk the loss of a few trifles for an eternal crown? Shall they risk the loss of eternal friends, such as God to love, Christ to redeem, the Holy Spirit to comfort, heaven for a habitation, saints and angels for company; and all this to get and hold communion with sin, and this world, and a few base, drunken, swearing, lying, covetous wretches like themselves? And shall we not labour as hard, run as fast, seek as diligently, no, a hundred times more diligently, for the company of these glorious, eternal friends, though with the loss of such as these, no, with the loss of ten thousand times better than these poor, low, base, contemptible things? Shall it be said, at the last day, that wicked men made more haste to hell than you did make to heaven? Shall it be said that they spent more hours, days, and early and late at that, for hell than you spent for that which is ten thousand, thousand of thousands times better? Oh, let it not be so, but run with all 'might and main'. So, you see, I have here spoken something, though but little. Now I shall come to make some use and application of what has been said and so conclude.

# $I\mathcal{V}$

## Nine uses of this subject

### *The first use*

You see here that he who would go to heaven must run for it. Yes, and not only run, but so run — that is, as I have said, to run earnestly, to run continually, to strip off everything that would hinder in his race with the rest. Well, then, do you run in this way? And now let us examine this a little more.

1. Have you got into the right way? Are you in Christ's righteousness? Do not say, 'Yes,' in your heart, when in truth there is no such thing. It is a dangerous thing, you know, for a man to think he is in the right way when he is in the wrong one. It is the best way for him to lose his way, and not only that, but if he runs for heaven, as you say you do, then it is the best way to lose that too! Oh, this is the misery of most men, to persuade themselves that they are running correctly when they have never had one foot in the way! May the Lord give you understanding here, or else you are undone for ever. I beg you, soul, examine when it was that you turned from your sins and self-righteousness into the righteousness of Jesus Christ. I say, do you see yourself in him? Is he more precious to you than the whole world? Is your mind always meditating on him? Do you love to be

talking about him and also to be walking with him? Do you consider his company to be more precious than the whole world? Do you consider all things to be but poor, lifeless, vain things, without communion with him? Does his company sweeten all things, and his absence embitter all things? Soul, I beg you, be serious and take it to heart, and do not presume upon things of such weighty concern as the salvation or damnation of your soul without good ground.

2. Have you unburdened yourself of the things of this world, such as pride, pleasures, profits, lusts, vanities? What, do you think you can run fast enough with the world, your sins and lusts in your heart? I tell you, soul, those who have laid all aside every weight, every sin, and have got into the nimblest posture, they find it work enough to run, to run so as to keep going. To run through all that opposition, all the jostles, all the rubs, over all the stumbling blocks, over all the snares, from all the entanglements that the devil, sin, the world and their own hearts lay before them. I tell you, if you are going heavenward, you will find it no small or easy matter. Have you therefore discharged and unburdened yourself of these things? Never talk of going to heaven if you have not. It is to be feared you will be found among the many who 'will seek to enter and will not be able' (Luke 13:24).

### The second use

If so, in the next place, what will become of those who have grown weary before they have got halfway there? Why, man, it is he who holds out to the end who must be saved. It is he who overcomes who shall inherit all things; it is not everyone who begins who gets there in the end. Agrippa suddenly took a good step — he almost stepped into the bosom of Christ in less than half an hour. 'You,' he says to

Paul, 'almost persuade me to become a Christian' (Acts
26:28). Ah, but it was only *almost*, and so he had as good as
if he had never had anything at all. He stepped well, indeed,
but yet he stepped short. He was hot while he was at it, but
he was quickly out of wind. Oh, this *but almost*! I tell you,
this *but almost* lost him his soul! I think I have seen sometimes how these poor sinners who get *but almost* to heaven,
how fearfully their *almost*, their *but almost* will torment
them in hell, when they shall cry out in the bitterness of
their soul, saying, '*Almost* a Christian. I *almost* got into the
kingdom; I was *almost* out of the hands of the devil, *almost*
out of my sins, *almost* out from under the curse of God,
*almost*, and that was all, a*lmost*, but not altogether.' Oh,
that I should be *almost* at heaven and should not quite go
in. Friend, it is a sad thing to sit down before we are in
heaven and to grow weary before we come to the place of
rest. And if this should be your case, I am sure you do not
run so as to obtain. But again,

### The third use

In the next place, what then will become of them that some
time ago were running post-haste to heaven, inasmuch as
they seemed to outstrip many, but are now running as fast
back again? Do you think these will ever get there? What,
to run back again! To run back again to sin, to the world, to
the devil, back again to the lusts of the flesh? Oh, 'It would
have been better for them not to have known the way of
righteousness, than having known it, to turn from the holy
commandment delivered to them' (2 Peter 2:21). Those men
shall not only be damned for sin, but for professing to all
the world that sin is better than Christ. For the man who
runs back again does as good as say, 'I have tried Christ and
I have tried sin, and I do not find as much profit in Christ

as in sin.' I say, this man declares this by running back again. Oh, what a sad thing! What doom they will have who were almost at heaven's gates and then ran back again! 'But if anyone draws back,' says Christ, 'my soul has no pleasure in him' (Heb. 10:38). Again, 'No one, having put his hand to the plough [that is, having set forward in the ways of God] and looking back [turning back again], is fit for the kingdom of God' (Luke 9:62). And if he is not fit for the kingdom of heaven, then for certain he must needs be fit for the fire of hell. 'And, therefore,' says the apostle, 'those who bring forth these apostatizing fruits, "if it bears thorns and briars, it is rejected and near to being cursed, whose end is to be burned"' (Heb. 6:8). Oh, there is never another Christ to save them by bleeding and dying for them! And if those who neglect shall not escape, how, then, shall they escape that reject and turn their back upon 'so great a salvation'? If the righteous — that is, those who run for it, will find it work enough to get to heaven, 'Where will the ungodly [backslider] and the sinner appear?' (1 Peter 4:18). Or, if Judas, the traitor, or Francis Spira, the backslider, were now alive in the world to whisper in the ear of these men a little and to tell them what backsliding has cost their souls, surely it would stick with them and make them afraid of running back again as long as they had one day to live in this world.

### The fourth use

So again, fourthly, how unfamiliar to these men's passions will those be who have all this while sat still, and have not so much as set one foot in the direction of the kingdom of heaven! Surely he who backslides and he who sits still in sin are both of one mind. The one will not stir because he loves his sins and the things of this world; the other runs back again because he loves his sins and the things of this world. Is it not one and the same thing? They are all one here; and shall not one and the same hell hold them hereafter? He is an ungodly person who never looked to Christ; and he is an ungodly person who did once look to him and then ran right back again. Therefore, that word must certainly fall from the mouth of Christ against them both, 'Depart from me, you cursed, into the everlasting fire prepared for the devil and his angels' (Matt. 25:41).

## The fifth use

Again, here you may see, in the next place, that those who will obtain heaven must run for it. This then calls aloud to those who began just a while ago to run, I say, they should mend their pace if they intend to win. You know that those who are at the rear need to run fastest. Friend, I tell you, there are those who have run for ten years to your one, no, twenty to your five, and yet if you talk with them sometimes they will say they doubt they shall come late enough. How then will it be with you? Look to it therefore that you delay no longer, not an hour's time, but part speedily with everything that is a hindrance to you in your journey, and run. Yes, run in such a way that you may obtain.

## The sixth use

Again, sixthly, you who have professed faith for a long time, take heed that the young followers of Jesus, who began to follow just the other day, do not outrun you, so as to have that scripture fulfilled in you, 'Many who are first will be last, and the last first' (Matt. 19:30), which will be a shame to you and a credit to them. What, for a young soldier to be more courageous than he who has been used to wars! To

you who are coming up the rear, I say, strive to outrun those
who are ahead of you. And to you who are in front, I say,
hold your ground and keep ahead of them in faith and love,
if possible. For indeed that is the right running: for one to
strive to outrun another, even for him who is right behind
to endeavour to overtake him who is right in front; and he
who is ahead should be sure to extend himself to keep his
ground, even to the utmost. But then,

### The seventh use

How basely do they behave themselves, how unlikely are
they to win, who think it enough to keep company with
those at the rear! There are some men who profess themselves to be those who run for heaven as well as any, yet if
there are but any lazy, slothful, cold, half-hearted professing believers in the country, they will be sure to take their
example from them. They think that if they can but keep
pace with them, then they shall do all right. But these people
do not consider that those at the rear lose the prize. You
may know it, if you will, that it cost the foolish virgins dear
for their coming too late: 'And those who were ready went
in with him to the wedding; and the door was shut. Afterwards [note, *afterwards*] the other [foolish] virgins came
also, saying, "Lord, Lord, open to us!" But he answered and
said, "Assuredly, I say to you, I do not know you"' (Matt.
25:10-12). Depart lazy professing believers, cold professing believers, slothful professing believers. Oh, I think the
Word of God is so clear about the overthrow of those lazy
professing believers that it is to be wondered men do not
take more notice of it. How was Lot's wife dealt with for
running lazily and for giving but one look behind her at
the things she left in Sodom? How was Esau dealt with for
waiting too long before he came for the blessing? And how

were they dealt with who are mentioned in Luke 13:25 for waiting till the door was shut? Also, the foolish virgins, a heavy after-groan will they give who have thus waited too long. It turned Lot's wife into a pillar of salt (Gen 19:26). It made Esau weep with an exceedingly loud and bitter cry (Heb. 12:17). It made Judas hang himself. Yes, and it will make you curse the day in which you were born if you miss the kingdom, as you will certainly do if this is your course. But,

### The eighth use

Again, how, and if you by your lazy running should not only destroy yourself, but also thereby be the cause of the damnation of some others! For you being a professing believer must recognize that others will take notice of you. And because you are but a poor, cold, lazy runner, and one who seeks to drive the world and pleasure along with you, why, thereby others will think of doing so too. 'No,' they say, 'why may we not do as he? He is a professing believer, and yet he seeks after pleasures, riches, profits. He loves vain company, and he is proud, and he is so and so, and claims that he is going to heaven. Yes, and he says also that he does not fear that he shall not be well received. Let us therefore keep pace with him; we shall fare no worse than he.' Oh, how fearful a thing will it be if you are instrumental in the ruin of others by your halting in the way of righteousness! Look to it! You will have little enough strength to appear before God to give an account of the loss of your own soul! You need not have to give an account for others, as to why you stopped them from entering in. How will you answer those words, 'You would not enter in yourselves, and those who would, you hinder'? For those words will be eminently fulfilled in those who through their own idleness keep themselves out of heaven, and, by giving to others the same example, hinder them also.

*The ninth use*

Therefore, now to speak a word to both of you, and, in this way, I shall conclude.

1. I plead with you in the name of our Lord Jesus Christ that none of you run so lazily in the way to heaven that you hinder either yourselves or others. I know that even he who runs in the laziest fashion, should he see a man running for a temporal life who should so much neglect his own well-being in this world as to risk it, when he is running, to pick up here and there a lock of wool that hangs by the wayside, or to step now and then aside out of the way in order to gather up a straw or two, or any rotten stick — I say, if he should do this when he is a running for his life, you would condemn him. And do you not condemn yourself who do the very same thing in effect, no, worse — you loiter in your race, notwithstanding the fact that your soul, heaven, glory, and all is at stake! Have a care, have a care, poor, wretched sinner! Have a care!

2. If there are still any, notwithstanding this advice, who will still be flagging and loitering in the way to the kingdom of glory, be so wise as not to follow their example. Learn of no man further than he follows Christ. But look to Jesus, who is not only the author and finisher of faith, but who, for the joy that was set before him, endured the cross, despising the shame, and has now sat down at the right hand of God. I say, look to no man to learn from him further than he follows Christ. 'Be ye followers of me,' says Paul, 'even as I also am of Christ' (1 Cor. 11:1, AV). Though he was an eminent man, yet his exhortation was that none should follow him any further than he followed Christ.

# *VI*

## A final exhortation

Well, then, sinner, what do you say? Where is your heart? Will you run? Are you resolved to run, or are you not? Think quickly, man, it is not a matter to dally with. Confer not with flesh and blood. Look up to heaven, and see how you like it; also to hell — of which you may understand something in my book, called *A Few Sighs from Hell*, or, *The Groans of a Damned Soul*, which I wish you to read seriously — and devote yourself accordingly. If you do not know the way, inquire from the Word of God. If you lack company, cry for God's Spirit. If you lack encouragement, consider the promises. But be sure you begin early; get into the way; run apace; and hold out to the end; and may the Lord give you a prosperous journey!

Farewell.

$\mathcal{V}$

## Exhortation to run with those at the front

Now, that you may be exhorted to run with those at the front, take note of this: when Lot and his wife were running from cursed Sodom to the mountains to save their lives, it is said that his wife looked back from behind him, and she became a pillar of salt. And yet, you see that neither her practice, nor the judgement of God that fell upon her for this deed, would cause Lot to look behind him. I have sometimes wondered at Lot in this incident: his wife looked behind her and died immediately; but, whatever became of her, Lot would not so much as look behind him to see her. We do not read that he so much as once looked back to see where she was or what had become of her. His heart was indeed upon his journey, as well it could have been. There was the mountain before him, and the fire and brimstone behind him; his life lay at stake and he would have lost it if he had but looked behind him. See to it that you run in the same way. And in your race remember Lot's wife, remember her doom, remember for what that doom overtook her, and remember that God has made her an example for all lazy runners to the end of the world; and take heed that you do not fall in the same manner. But if this will not stir you up, consider thus:

1. Your soul is your own soul, either to be saved or lost — you shall not lose *my* soul by your laziness. It is your own soul, your own ease, your own peace, your own advantage or disadvantage. If it were my soul that you desired to be good to, I think reason should move you somewhat to pity it. But, alas, it is your own, your own soul: 'For what will it profit a man if he gains the whole world, and loses his own soul?' (Mark 8:36). God's people wish well to the souls of others, and will you not wish well to your own? And if this will not stir you up, then think again,

2. If you lose your soul, it is you who must also bear the blame. It made Cain stark mad to consider that he had not looked to his brother Abel's soul. How much more will it perplex you to think that you had not a care of your own? And if this will not cause you to stir yourself, think again,

3. That if you will not run, the people of God are resolved to deal with you even as Lot dealt with his wife — that is, leave you behind them. It may be you have a father, mother, brother, etc. going post-haste to heaven. Would you be willing to be left behind them? Surely not! Again,

4. Will it not be a dishonour to you to see that the boys and girls in the country have more sense than you? It may be the servants of some men, such as the horsekeeper, ploughman, servant, etc. are looking more towards heaven than their masters. Sometimes, I am inclined to think that more servants than masters, more tenants than landlords will inherit the kingdom of heaven. But is this not a shame for those that are such? I am persuaded that you would scorn the idea that your servants should say that they are wiser than you in the things of this world; and yet, I am bold enough to say that many of them are wiser than you in the things of the world to come, which are of greater concern.